LOOKING FORWARD

Dave Jette
January 23, 2021

CONTENTS

INTRODUCTION

Commencing in February 2020 I have written a bi-monthly column "Looking Forward" in the progressive monthly newspaper *Works in Progress* published in Olympia, Washington. This book gives all of these columns: the six which have already been published, and additional draft columns which are expected to be published (not necessarily in the order given).

In addition, as appendices four essays are given: "Socialists' Tasks in an Anti-Right Front: Reply to Calvin Cheung-Miaw", which is an elaboration of Column 7; "Defeating Trumpism", an elaboration of Column 12; "The Partisan Experience", which the author had in the early 1970's in Canada; and "The Washington State Rainbow Coalition", a major struggle in which the author was involved in 1989.

The author has self-published two other books recently. **A Reformulation of Dialectical Materialism**, in 2019, incorporates feminist theory into the traditional Marxist presentation of the science of dialectical materialism, with an appendix which discusses the question of whether nature exhibits dialectical development, demonstrating that non-living phenomena (such as described by the sciences of physics and chemistry) are definitely not dialectical, in contradiction to traditional Marxist theory. **Beyond Classical Marxism**, published in 2020, is about socialism and how to work to bring it about in the United States. The present book, as well as the two previous books, are available at Lulu Press (www.lulu.com). In addition, the author maintains a political website at www.bcmsocialism.org which provides much of the material in these three books.

The author is much indebted to Max Elbaum for his critical feedback on drafts of some of these essays, and to Bethany Weidner and the rest of the *Works in Progress* editorial team for their strong encouragement of the "Looking Forward" columns.

The author, living in Seattle, can be contacted at dave@jettes.org.

Column 1: Introduction.
Published in February 2020.

*[Beginning with this issue, Dave Jette's bi-monthly column will review possibilities for urgent collective action to confront the threat of fascism and the collapse of human habitat. Dave has been involved with Works in Progress since its beginnings, writing an early column and recently contributing occasional articles. He is the author of **A Reformation of Dialectical Materialism**, which incorporates feminist theory into a traditional Marxist framework (available at www.lulu.com).]*

Our civilization is at a crossroads, with the threat of fascism both in our country and throughout the world, as well as that of the collapse of human habitat due to global warming. The seriousness of the situation facing us cannot be underestimated. It is imperative that we have a solid grasp of what is going on and how we can (and must!) reshape the future.

In "Looking Forward" I intend to inform readers of the possibilities for and necessity of effective collective action to save our civilization. This column will relate the insights and analyses of progressives similarly concerned about prospects for the future, as well as my own views. As I shall elucidate in this column, socialism offers the only humane alternative to the manifold depredations of capitalist society, and I have recently joined the (national) socialist organization Solidarity.

In this column, I'll cover topics that provide a grounding for the current situation as well as those that concern ways in which people can work together to effect the necessary new social relations. The primary purpose of this work will be to facilitate people taking this transformation into their own hands to build a multi-faceted democratic mass movement. Below are some topics which this column will be addressing:

1. To what extent is what Donald Trump is promoting in our own country, as well as new authoritarian governments elsewhere, really fascism (or "neofascism")? What is the relationship of the capitalist class to these movements, and to the full implementation of fascism?

2. What are the various "socialist" organizations operating in the United States, such as the Green Party, the Democratic Socialists of America (DSA) with some 60,000 members, and Socialist Alternative which has placed and twice retained one of its members, Kshama Sawant, on the Seattle City Council? I shall provide information about who they are and what they stand for and do, for the benefit of persons who may be interested in working with them.

3. What should be the relationship of socialist activists to the Democratic Party, which for untold decades has functioned to enfeeble and absorb progressive struggles?

4. What are the critical environmental issues facing us, and what organizations are vigorously involved in addressing them? How can people (nonviolently) support legal and extra-legal struggles against environmental devastation?

5. Who is so strongly against LGBT rights? Although in the United States many Catholics are supportive of such

rights, the Catholic Church gives them only lip service, and in Africa, for example, it stands in the forefront of opposition to such persons. In the U.S. white Evangelical Christians are adamantly opposed to LGBT rights. How can progressives turn many of these people around?

6. How can socialists help unite people in an informal coalition to overcome white supremacy, while still vigorously promoting socialism as the only solution to our society's fundamental ills? What is the relationship of (economic) class to the promotion of white supremacy?

7. What will happen if Trump refuses to leave office, either after successful impeachment or by losing the coming presidential election? Early in his term Trump said that he may be forced by his followers to remain in office even if he loses re-election. How can progressives help organize mass struggles to overthrow Trump's installation as an outright dictator?

8. What organizational forms can be effective for convincing Americans to support the full range of socialist measures? To what extent is it true that the more disciplined and better structured an organization is, the better will be its chances of becoming effective in building a progressive democratic mass movement? How useful is the Leninist concept of "democratic centralism?" (It is arguable that the involvement of *any* disciplined organization is antithetical to building such a mass movement.)

9. What are the prospects for the indefinite continuation of capitalism in its present form ("neoliberalism"), and are

other forms of capitalism currently possible? The destruction of our environment is due overwhelmingly to our capitalist economic system, at least in its present form; capitalists must necessarily produce more and more in order to survive, and their control of our political system enables them to do so.

10. What does genuine socialism entail, which people should be striving for? What is its relationship to social democracy, as espoused for example by Bernie Sanders? "Socialism" is a broad term for a system of social relations supplanting capitalism, and it is important to understand what is possible and necessary in advocating for this transformed social system.

Column 2: Socialism
Published in April 2020.

What is socialism? As capitalism developed, ethically outraged people proposed various alternatives to its depravities, typically terming their suggested models "socialism". But these models, dismissed as being "petit-bourgeois socialism" by Marxists, have long been superseded by the "scientific socialism" of Marx and Engels based on Marx's rigorous analysis of capitalism and the philosophical theory of dialectical materialism.

There are three main camps of followers of Marx:

1. Social democracy (the Second International)
2. Stalinism (the Third International), based on the experience of the Soviet Union and adhering to "Marxism-Leninism"
3. Trotskyism (the Fourth International), adhering to "Marxism-Leninism" as interpreted by Trotsky

I have some fundamental differences with all these Marxist versions of socialism, and after explaining these differences I shall list what I consider to be the defining characteristics of the "socialism" which we should strive for.

Problems with Marxism-Leninism

1. The one-party state is inimical to democracy, and it must be possible to vote the "socialist government" out of office. This means that people must be able to organize opposition, although the use of large amounts of wealth must be prevented. Cuba, for example, provides very well for its people, and it is far more democratic than the U.S. in responding to the desires of the populace, but it is nonetheless top-down politically – not socialist.

2. The role of the state can be highly positive, in facilitating – not dominating! – people's building a just, liberated society. The Marxist goal of the "withering away of the state" (in the eventual "communist" society) is simply wrong.

3. The concept of the "dictatorship of the proletariat" is wrong in negating the vital role of the middle classes in building the socialist society. Society is a lot more complex than it was in Marx's day, when it was clearly dominated by the struggle between the capitalists and the working class. Furthermore, this concept leads straight to the rule of society by the politically advanced "party of the working class" on behalf of the workers themselves.

4. Traditional Marxism greatly overemphasizes the role of economic struggles between the capitalists and the working class in transforming society. Left out (until recently) are non-economic struggles for a decent life, such as against racism, the oppression of

women, and homophobia. Also left out is the vital role of the middle classes, which must actively participate in the struggle for socialism.

5. Overall, Marxism-Leninism provides serious revolutionaries with ready-made formulas for political work. Unfortunately, they have strongly tended to just follow what is presented as "scientific socialism" rather than to question and overcome its weaknesses.

Problems with social democracy

1. Social democracy has a Marxist orientation, but it leaves capitalism in place while trying to control it. In particular, it leaves the "commanding heights of the economy" (big banks, huge corporations) in the hands of the capitalists so that they remain in effect the (political) ruling class. While living conditions may well be improved for the masses, fundamental social change is impossible under social democracy.

2. The primary allegiance of social democrats is to the capitalists, making sure that the economy functions properly, rather than to humankind throughout the world. Accordingly, when push comes to shove they will side with their country (*i.e.*, with "their" capitalists) in building and maintaining the Empire. This is exactly what happened in World War I.

3. Bernie Sanders is a social democrat, not a socialist, but what he has been advocating constitutes a major, progressive change in American politics. While not mitigating their own politics, socialists should support his current presidential campaign as a step forward in a highly reactionary situation.

Defining characteristics of socialism

1. Socialism means complete democracy – not "top-down" government. There is no such thing as "undemocratic socialism".
2. People must take into their own hands the building of a multi-faceted democratic mass movement to transform society into a socialist one, rather than having it done for them by government or by "advanced" political parties.
3. An essential role in the creation of the new society must be played by the middle classes.
4. Control by society of the big financial institutions and corporations must be eliminated by nationalizing them (with financial compensation given to their owners).
5. Full play must be given to all struggles for human rights, such as against racism, the oppression of women, and homophobia.
6. Socialists must vociferously oppose imperialist wars to build and maintain the American Empire, and give support to peoples subject to American economic and military domination.

7. As a highest priority, socialists must work to combat
   the climate change which is on the verge of
   destroying our ecosystem.

Column 3: Miliband's Practical Model of Socialism.
Published in June 2020.

The previous column explained what socialism
is and what it isn't. However, to effect actual change,
we need something concrete to advocate for and
organize around. Without a shared map, so to speak, of
the territory, the abstract idea of adopting socialist
principles remains pie in the sky. The long censorship
of the idea of socialism (to say nothing of
communism) in the U.S. has diminished the resources
available for collectively imagining our future.

Fortunately, a concrete model has been worked
out in great detail by the British intellectual Ralph
Miliband in his book **Socialism for a Sceptical Age**
(Verso, 1994). It is the subject of this column, and I
consider it to be fully appropriate, which is not to say
that other models based on socialism as defined in the
last column are not also valid.

Miliband presents a model of a mixed economy
which is considered to be the end of the society which
socialists should be striving for, not some sort of
transitional society to a higher stage (e.g.
"communism"): "A socialized economy would consist
of three distinct sectors. First, there would be a
predominant and varied public sector. Secondly, there
would exist a substantial and expanding cooperative
sector. Thirdly, there would endure a sizable privately
owned sector, mainly made up of small and medium

firms, with an important part to play in the provision of goods, services, and amenities" (p. 110).

The public sector in this model includes state ownership of the banking and financial system and of the immense corporations which presently combine to control our political system for the benefit of the extremely wealthy ("the 1%"). State ownership ("nationalization") would be acquired not by outright confiscation, but through compensation "by way of the issue of government bonds, redeemable over an extended period of time; and a considerable degree of differentiation would also have to be made between small and large investors, with facilities for more rapid redemption available to small investors" (pp. 109-110).

The public sector would also include regional and local activities undertaken by regional and municipal authorities, particularly in the provision of services and amenities such as transportation, electricity, water and sewage, daycare centers, and community centers, to name but a few such activities. Such economic activities are often already "owned" by the public, but under neoliberalism they are increasingly being privatized so that the wealthy can squeeze even more money out of the public.

Public enterprises would have a considerable degree of autonomy, unlike the bureaucratic Soviet system of rigid, top-down planning. Nonetheless, the government would be able to intervene in their activities – sparingly applied – "to ensure compliance with its macroeconomic policies and objectives, and with its concerns about health and safety, employment, and the rights of workers" (p. 110). Furthermore, there must be "the greatest possible degree of participation in the determination of policy by everyone employed in the enterprise who wishes to be involved, and the attribution of real power to employees in regard to all issues which directly affect them – for instance, health and safety, the process of production, conditions of work, etc." (p. 111).

Regarding the cooperative sector of a socialist economy, Miliband calls for the government to actively strengthen it, in the field of production as well as distribution, and in the provision of services. He points out that such enterprises now play a very subsidiary role in capitalist economies.

Finally, a wide range of small and medium-sized firms, individually owned and controlled, would comprise a sizable sector of the economy. Their existence would be considered a permanent feature in this version of a socialist economy. According to Miliband, the inclusion of a private sector "introduces an additional element of competition in the provision of goods, services, and amenities. It gives the opportunity to individuals who are so inclined to try their hand at independent ventures, and to experiment with new products and services. A socialist regime would not only find this acceptable, but would actively encourage such individual initiatives. But it would at the same time see to it that the private sector remained a subsidiary part of the economy as a whole" (p. 113).

All of these economic enterprises would be subject to competition from each other. A critical proposition in this model is that the economy is regulated. As Miliband puts it, in our current system, market forces are the ultimate determiners of economic life. Government and the society which sustains it have handed responsibility for deciding what needs to be done for the common good and the achievements of social justice to these "market forces" and the private interests they represent. The mixed economy model described by Milibrand makes a critical shift by subordinating the economy to the government and the society it represents.

This column can only introduce some salient aspects of Miliband's model of socialism; to really understand it, one should read his book, especially its fourth chapter. But even in skeletal form, this model provides a coherent conceptual model and a solid answer about what socialism could mean in real life, and how it could be politically practical to embark on such a fundamental transformation of our present capitalist economy.

Column 4: Trump and Fascism

Is President Donald Trump leading us into fascism? To consider this question, it is necessary top understand the role which fascism plays in a capitalist society, why the capitalist class turns to facilitating the rise of fascism. Such understanding is provided in the collection of essays **Radical Perspectives on the Rise of Fascism in Germany, 1919-1945** (Monthly Review Press, 1989).

In the aftermath of World War I, a democratic parliamentary political system was set up in defeated Germany, as the "Weimar Republic". The capitalists were divided into three major factions: heavy industry (iron, steel, mining) focused on domestic economic development; export industry (dynamic, technologically more advanced, and more prosperous) led by machine, electric, and chemical industries as well as textiles and commercial interests; and agriculture (the landed aristocracy, particularly the "Junkers" of Prussia). The "middle class" consisted of shopkeepers, commodity producers, and salaried employees, as well as the peasantry). The working class had strong labor unions and a strong political party (the Social Democratic Party of Germany, or "SPD") and a German Communist Party ("KPD") which had been greatly weakened by the abortive revolutionary uprisings following World War I.

At first the export-industry fraction of the bourgeoisie was dominant in representing capital, and the labor unions and SPD were able to work with this fraction in considerably improving workers' lives, until 1930. They were, in fact, "too" successful, for heavy industry was then unable to make a decent profit and the economic system was in major distress. In the early 1930's heavy industry achieved hegemony over the export industry and refused to collaborate politically with workers' organizations. However, the political system was so dysfunctional that the Weimar parliament lost most mass support in spite of efforts by heavy industry to revive it. The only really strong political parties in the early 1930's were the fascist NSDAP (the National Socialist German Workers Party of Hitler, based most strongly in the "middle class") and the SPD (with some help from the KPD, although at this time the communists were denouncing the social democrats as being the main enemy of the revolution). So the capitalists tried to use the NSDAP as a junior partner in parliament, as a substitute for their lack of mass following. But Hitler refused any deal other than one making him Chancellor, and the capitalists finally capitulated, especially since the NSDAP in the most recent election appeared to be in decline and there was the danger that it would fade away.

So on January 30, 1933 Hitler was appointed Chancellor of Germany. He quickly destroyed the labor unions and soon all other political parties, using as necessary the huge army of streetfighters (the SA, or "stormtroopers") which the NSDAP had built up. Through a referendum he had himself and his party declared the sole ruler of Germany, and by 1938 he had replaced the old state bureaucracy with his own followers. Anti-Semitism was eagerly implemented in Germany, with Jews deprived of any political or social influence and even of their livelihood; this treatment was but a prelude to the Holocaust which the Germans carried out in eastern Europe as soon as they were able to, when Germany invaded Poland in September 1939.

Furthermore, analysis for understanding authoritarianism in the United States aids in comprehending the possibilities for implementing fascism here. A comrade has kindly provided the following analysis of authoritarianism here, the key reference points being slavery, the Civil War, the rollback of Reconstruction, Jim Crow, and changing demographics as a major stress for the contemporary period. The next column will then consider the question of to what extent Trump is implementing fascism in the United States.

In the pre-Civil-War period and the Civil War, a whole section of society, anchored in the slaveowners but extending to a cross-class white bloc, viewed their whole civilization and "way of life" as being dependent on maintaining slavery. So they used "any means necessary" to try to defend and expand it. They were beaten, but came back via racist terror and the assault on Black voting rights to roll back Reconstruction and put in place Jim Crow for a hundred years. This was essentially apartheid – Blacks in the South "had no rights the white man needed to respect" and this was enforced through lynching – *i.e.* through open terror.

Now we are living through another stage in the rollback of the gains of the 1960's (and of the 30's as well). And for the first time since the Civil War, a whole layer of society – again rooted in the most reactionary sectors of capital but extending to a cross-class white bloc – believes (since because of demographic change, the U.S. in 30-40 years will be a majority people-of-color country) that if democracy and majority rule exists in the U.S., their whole way of life (white Christian American civilization) will go under. So they are prepared to – more than that, enthusiastic to – set in place a system for long-term rule by a minority of the population via authoritarian means. Big sectors of capital – not all, but highly important ones such as energy corporations and the military-industrial complex – are behind this because they know their ecoholic and energy policies (climate change denialism) are unpopular not just with communities of color but also with young whites.

So there is a massive force moving toward what could be called neo-apartheid, a racialized authoritarian state, "illiberal democracy" or even a not-classical-European fascism but still essentially a form of fascism. This may occur even in the absence of a strong communist or revolutionary left. This is what Trumpism is about: the absolute determination of roughly 30% of the U.S. population right now to turn to explicit authoritarianism in which immigrants and Blacks are not "real Americans" and have no rights that the "real Americans" need to respect.

Column 4a: More on Trump and Fascism
(This was meant to be a continuation of Column 4, but it was postponed and then never published.)

Is President Donald Trump promoting fascism in the United States? With the August column's understanding of the rise of fascism in Germany and the history of authoritarianism in our own country, let us first look at the ways in which it is valid to say that Trump is doing this:

1. Trump is building up a mass following based on explicit calls for white supremacy. (The Republican Party has long been implicitly based on white supremacy, starting with Nixon's "Southern strategy"; he is raising use of this noxious ideology to a new level.)

2. Another critical component of building a mass reactionary following is Trump's clearly stated misogyny.

3. Trump viciously attacks "The Other", in this case immigrants of color and Moslems. This corresponds with the Nazis's using Jews and Slavs (non-Aryans) as their scapegoats.

4. Trump expresses utter contempt for persons who oppose or disagree with him.

5. Trump engages in blatant lying, knowing full well that doing this will be accepted by his mass base.

6. Trump attacks the mass media, whether conservative or liberal, as "the enemy of the people".

7. Trump dismisses as "fake news" whatever evidence contradicts his pronouncements, including undeniable scientific conclusions. He promotes total distrust for science and the scientific method. Thus with this and the preceding three points he has been building up a mass of followers who mindlessly accept whatever pronouncement he chooses to make.

8. Trump completely disregards the rule of law whenever it suits him. In fact, early in his tenure he stated that if he were voted out of office, he might have to obey the wishes of his followers in their insistence that he remain in office.

9. Trump promotes public demonstrations of armed, far-right-wing "patriots" in support of his policies.

On the other hand, there are important ways in which Trump does not go beyond staunch conservatism towards outright fascism:

1. Trump is not building up a disciplined mass party like Hitler's NSDAP.

2. Trump is not creating organized militias like the Nazis's SA stormtroopers.

3. Trump has little support of much of the major economic elite. They are not yet needing him as

Supreme Leader with mass support, as heavy
industry did in the early 1930's in Germany.

4. Trump gives strong support for military spending,
   but not for entanglement in foreign wars. (One of
   the few positive things that one can say about
   Trump's conduct!)

5. Trump gives strong support for maintenance of the
   U.S. empire, especially regarding Israel, but this is
   what the Republicans and mainstream Democrats
   do anyway.

6. Trump provides basically nominal support for
   Christian conservatism, but not including blatant
   religious fervor such as that expressed in anti-
   Semitism.

7. Trump also provides nominal support for anti-
   LGBTQ activity, but not to the extent of making
   such persons "The Other".

So what can one conclude from this analysis? It
would be wrong to charge Trump with systematically
bringing about fascism, for that is only going to
happen when a fundamental economic crisis occurs
and the economic elite find it necessary to use the
mass base provided by demagogues like Trump to
destroy our outwardly democratic processes in order to
effect a fascist dictatorship. But it *is* reasonable to
recognize that Trump is laying the *groundwork* (even
if unintentionally) for a future transformation to
fascism. This, as well as Trump's vigorous promotion

of climate change which will destroy the world, is why
it has been so critically important to deny him a second
term in office. (And the need for a fascist dictatorship
may be forthcoming sooner than one might think, for
neoliberalism is sinking capitalism into the ground
with no alternative in sight.)

Column 5: The Political Origins of *Works in Progress*

Published in October 2020.

Our story begins with the 1988 presidential campaign of Jesse Jackson. All around the country, "Rainbow Coalitions" were organized at the local and state level in support of the campaign. In Washington state, there thus came into being an incipient state Rainbow Coalition with various components including the Thurston County Rainbow Coalition (TCRC).

In the aftermath of the November 1988 election various efforts were made to create ongoing Rainbow Coalitions. Here the state Rainbow Coalition under the leadership of Larry Gossett decided to hold a founding convention in February. Jackson, who had plans other than creating semi-autonomous democratic progressive electoral organizations, asked us to refrain from doing so, but we ignored his request not to hold our founding convention and went ahead with doing so.

At this time I was elected one of seven officers (Corresponding Secretary) of the newly formed Washington State Rainbow Coalition (WSRC). Organizationally, we got off to an excellent start, with top leadership being mainly persons of color; the WSRC Executive Committee ("ExCom", consisting of the seven officers) had only two white persons including me.

However, in early March Jackson and his National Rainbow Coalition (NRC) tried to rein in the incipient local and state Rainbow Coalitions around the country by imposing on them a totally authoritarian, top-down organizational structure with the NRC able to appoint or remove any state or even local officer, to determine the state organizational structure, and to (only) call state conventions. Alone within the WSRC ExCom, I vigorously opposed this transformation of the WSRC, and I forced a statewide meeting of WSRC members by circulating the new NRC bylaws to the various local components. (Fortunately, as Corresponding Secretary I had the addresses of all the local officers and was able to do this, to the anguish of the rest of the ExCom, who would have preferred to keep the membership in the dark about what was going on.) The result of this meeting was to keep the WSRC on its track of building a democratic organization from the ground up; this whole experience is detailed in my article "Washington State Rainbow" on my political website www.bcmsocialism.org, at https://bcmsocialism.org/the-washington-state-rainbow-coalition/.

Fast forward to the middle of 1990. The TCRC had started publishing, in June, its free monthly newspaper *Works in Progress* (*WiP*). There were also strong signs of life in Yakima, but otherwise the WSRC was steadily going downhill, with a membership which had dropped from over 1000 to around 300; people were just not renewing their membership, and the WSRC was becoming but a paper organization. The TCRC asked me to write a regular column for *WiP* commencing in September, which I was very happy to do in order, first, to try to save the WSRC by enlightening members as to what was going on.

So I drafted as my first column "The Rise and Fall of the Washington State Rainbow Coalition". It was rather far too long: it would have taken up three full pages of *WiP*. So we broke it up into two parts, with the first part giving the history and current status of the WSRC, particularly of its combatting the efforts of Jackson and the NRC to transform the WSRC into a component of Jackson's campaign organization, and with the second part (published in October as "Rebuilding the Vision") suggesting how we could resurrect the WSRC. Again fortunately, as Corresponding Secretary I maintained the membership role, so I gave *WiP* mailing labels and they sent the September issue out to all the remaining WSRC members.

Then the fun began, for the WSRC ExCom was aghast at my sending out on my own what they considered to be a trashing of the WSRC. I asked them for permission to send out the second part of the article, and although they were given the October issue, they didn't seem to accept that it was positive in trying to reinvigorate the organization and forbade me to do this. Instead, they "fired" me as Corresponding Secretary, which was illegal for them to do under our bylaws, and I just resigned from that position.

I then went from Seattle to a meeting of the TCRC and asked them to send out the October issue to all WSRC members in defiance of the WSRC ExCom. This they agreed almost unanimously to do. (One person wasn't happy with this course of action, but declined to block consensus.) A sheet accompanying that mailing started off with "You are not supposed to be getting this mailing!" and went on to explain that "we do not believe it is the proper role of the leadership of an organization to control, to filter, to restrict in any way, the flow of information and opinions to the members about what the organization is doing and how it is functioning".

The TCRC had passed its baptism of fire, speaking truth to power. The critical importance of a free, independent press had been well demonstrated. And the deep respect with which Larry Gossett and I held each other had been unaffected by these intense struggles within the WSRC: in 1993 I served on the campaign committee which placed this outstanding African-American leader on the King County Council for the first of 27 years.

Thus commenced my close relationship with *WiP*. In the first two years I published twenty columns

in my "On the Mark" series, mostly on theoretical
questions such as democracy, socialism, Marxism, etc.
Since then I published the occasional article in *WiP*,
and now, of course, I am writing the bi-monthly
column "Looking Forward". I should like to impress
on readers how politically significant the *WiP* project
has been, not only because of its unabashedly
progressive content, but also because in Washington
state it alone has survived for three decades, from the
ashes of the Washington State Rainbow Coalition. (In
Seattle there have been several attempts over the years
to create a progressive newspaper, but to no avail.)

Column 6: Doom and Gloom
Published in January 2021

I hate to spell out gloom and doom, but the fact
is that the presidential election demonstrated how
politically dangerous our situation in the United States
is. Sure, we did succeed in voting Donald Trump out
of office (although he does still appear to be preparing
for a violent coup), but only by the slimmest of
margins over a middle-of-the-road candidate who at
least paid lip service to some important progressive
issues. (Joe Biden seems forthright about mitigating
climate change, and he did call for addressing the
"original sin" of our country's founding on Black
slavery and indigenous peoples' genocide.) But
whereas, in 2016 one could hope that Trump would be
a decent, albeit conservative, president, in his four
years in office he has appealed to, and gained mass
support from, the worst of America: explicit white
supremacy, misogyny (particularly concerning
reproductive freedom), attacks on "The Other" (in this
case, immigrants of color and Moslems), attacks on the
mass media as "the enemy of the people", utter
contempt for persons who oppose or disagree with
him, blatant lying. He dismisses as "fake news"
whatever evidence contradicts his pronouncements,
including undeniable scientific conclusions, he
promoted irrational thinking through total distrust for
science and the scientific method, he completely
disregards the rule of law whenever it suits him, and he

promotes public demonstrations of armed, far-right-wing "patriots" in support of his policies.

Given Trump's outrageous rejection of professed American values and the financial support of much of the very wealthy as well as the support of the political/ideological "establishment" for Biden , it seems that the latter should have been a shoe-in for election as president. But the predicted Blue Wave came to naught: white women, white suburbanites, and white retirees did not desert Trump *en masse* and in fact the white electorate voted for Trump in the same percentage as in 2016 (57%). Probably Trump lost the election only because of his total mishandling of the Covid-19 pandemic, which ruined an otherwise bright economy.

So where does all this leave progressives and socialists seeking to transform our society into a humanly decent one? Politically, Trump was a bumbling fool, but the "Trumpism" accepted by almost half of the electorate remains. Capitalism, in its neoliberal version in the U.S., is in the process of disintegration, and will not the bourgeoisie be ready in 2024 to promote for president an autocratic, but highly competent, candidate like Pence or Pompeo, if need be? Hopefully the past presidential election will have woken up many of us who have treated the election as being just another instance of the "lesser of evils" trap, and fortunately their refusal to support Biden in closely contested "swing states" evidently has not

thrown the election to Trump even in states which
Biden won by a razor-thin margin, and in fact the
electorate has overwhelmingly rejected their
"politically correct" strategy. (In Washington State,
for example, the Green Party's Jill Stein took 1.82% of
the presidential vote in 2016, but this year their
candidate Howie Hawkins garnered only 0.44% of the
vote.) In this highly dangerous situation, let me
present two key ideas for what we may be able to do in
effectively countering our slide into autocracy and
possibly even outright fascism.

Progressive Mass Struggles. We are well
aware that the only way to fundamentally transform
our political/economic system in a progressive
direction is through mass struggle; electoral work can
be important in facilitating and strengthening such
struggles, but it cannot substitute for them. However,
we must disabuse ourselves of the notion, so ingrained
in classical Marxism, that it is basically the working
class that will undertake such struggles for a decent
life, that the amorphous "middle class" will have only
an auxiliary role to play. To the contrary, it is
individuals of both these classes that must have an
(equal) say in shaping the future society. Moreover, in
the U.S. huge portions of the working class accept and
even actively support Trumpism – where do you think
the bulk of Trump's over-70,000,000 votes just came
from? The role of progressives and socialists must be
to support and help develop the self-organization of

those working toward genuinely progressive social change regardless of their class.

Electoral Strategy. Building an independent progressive electoral party to challenge the hegemonic two-party system is, in the U.S. for the foreseeable future, a dead end. This is illustrated by the example of the Green Party with its excellent political platform and its organizational presence in most states; after decades of existence, it's clearly going nowhere, and in the just-concluded presidential election it might possibly have thrown the election to Trump with its candidate's challenging Biden in swing states. On the other hand, working within and seeking to transform the Democratic Party as the "lesser of evils" is also a fool's errand, for the Democratic Party just like the Republican Party is controlled by the bourgeoisie and its function for countless decades has been to absorb and destroy progressive struggles which threaten the economic system. What we propose to do is to *use* the Democratic Party to propagate our vision of a new society, as well as perhaps to take some steps towards fulfilling that vision, by supporting truly progressive candidates in primary elections of the Democratic Party. This by no means involves watering down our own politics in order (presumably) to win the primary, nor to fall into the trap of trying to transform the Democratic Party. Furthermore, we should play the game straight, in order not to (justifiably) be prevented from engaging in this tactic: if our candidate loses the primary, she/he should no longer be criticizing the

winner, and she/he may even support that person in the
general election if that person isn't clearly bad (such as
being anti-abortion); this is what Bernie Sanders
correctly did in the last two presidential elections.

Column 7: An Anti-Right Front? (draft)
(An elaboration of this essay is given as Appendix A.)

Trump is out, and Biden is in. Where do we go from here, in combatting the cancer of Trumpism and working toward the transformation of our society in a socialist direction? A very important essay on strategy for the coming years has recently been written by Calvin Cheung-Miaw and published by Organizing Upgrade: "The Pivot of U.S. Politics: Racial Justice and Democracy", www. https://organizingupgrade.com/the-pivot-of-u-s-politics-racial-justice-and-democracy/.

This essay stresses how intertwined the struggles for racial justice and democracy necessarily are: "Because of the predominant GOP strategy – uniting both Trumpists and the tepid old-guard conservatives of the party – is one of preserving its power through white minority rule, the struggle for racial justice is at the heart of the struggle for democracy. While those of us who were taught in the U.S. school system that U.S. democracy was the foundation of aspirations for racial equality, we should reverse this relationship. Historically and today, it is struggles for racial equality that have eroded the White Republic and produced what democracy we have in the U.S."

The ongoing danger of Trumpism cannot be underestimated. Since Election Day Trump has been claiming, without presenting any sort of proof, that the election was rigged, that he actually won hands down. A poll taken in November found that 77% of Republicans agree with him that the election was fraudulent: mindless people who follow *der führer* wherever he may lead them in safeguarding White Supremacy, and unfortunately a very substantial portion of the white working class! Perhaps 30% of the electorate are hard-right followers of Trump, accepting his outrageously blatant lies and his rejection of democracy and the rule of law. Presently they constitute a reserve force for the capitalists, to be used when society further crumbles as neoliberalism tanks. How possible is a transition to an outright authoritarian political system, or even to fascism?

Let us look at the example of Hitler's rise to power in Germany in 1933, as outlined in this column published last August (www.bcmsocialism.org/historical-fascism/. Unlike in the U.S. now, the various fractions of the bourgeoisie had lost most mass support in the parliament. "The only really strong political parties in the early 1930's were the fascist NSDAP (the National Socialist German Workers Party of Hitler, based most strongly in the 'middle class') and the Social Democratic Party of Germany (with some help from the German Communist Party, although at this time the communists were denouncing the social democrats as being the main enemy of the Revolution). So the capitalists tried to use the NSDAP as a junior partner in parliament, as a substitute for their lack of mass following. But Hitler refused any deal other than one making him Chancellor, and the capitalists finally capitulated, especially since the NSDAP in the most recent election appeared to be in decline and there was the danger that it would fade away." And so ended (bourgeois) democracy in Germany.

Is this where we are possibly headed? The Cheung-Miaw essay recognizes this great danger, and proposes the creation of an Anti-Right Front which includes not only progressives and socialists, but also moderate Democrats and even moderate Republicans who are willing to risk their political careers in order to combat the slide to Trumpism. The essay acknowledges that since racial justice issues tend to divide the anti-right front, "it will require some finesse to keep an anti-right front together under a Biden administration, but backing away from racial justice struggles will only weaken our long-term capacity to fight the forces pushing white minority rule". Thus the essay is advocating a sea-change in the way that socialists view the two-party system: the current outlook on the two-party system held by so many socialists, that we should have nothing to do with the Democratic Party (for very good reasons, of course!) is simply obsolete and counterproductive.

But an Anti-Right "Front"? This is certainly a tall order, and socialists can hardly expect to pull it off themselves. For the time being it must be informal, but still being engendered by our active participation in struggles for racial justice and democracy, linking them together (ideologically) as much as possible. It may eventually be useful to form an organization – at first basically a listserv for exchange of information and strategy – of progressives and socialists who are committed to this long-term project of building an anti-right front as expounded in this article, with emphasis on the struggle for racial justice as being essential to achieving democratic functioning. It is critical that those progressives and socialists who do agree with the anti-right front strategy start interacting more with each other, strategize together, and put other differences in proportion to the urgency of stopping fascism. Already we have the unfortunate example of the Democratic Socialists of America, the largest socialist group in the United States today, refusing to support Biden in order to combat the grave threat of Trumpism; socialists are simply going to have to give up their rigorous antipathy to having anything to do with the Democratic Party, if we are to survive.

(This is a shorter version of an article "Socialists' Tasks in an Anti-Right Front: Reply to Calvin Cheung-Miaw" published in January 2021 by Organizing Upgrade. It is available at https://organizingupgrade.com/socialists-tasks-in-an-anti-right-front-response-to-calvin-cheung-miaw/*.)*

Column 8: Lessons of "Imperium". (draft)

"Imperium" is a 2016 movie based on the real experiences of undercover FBI agent Mike German who infiltrated white supremacist organizations, as related in his book *Thinking Like a Terrorist* published in 2008. Unfortunately, the lessons found in the movie are all the more relevant today, as white-supremacist Trumpism increasingly gains strength in our country.

In the movie, after an automobile accident there is the disappearance of most of a shipment of containers of the radioactive substance cesium-137, used in treating cancer. The concern of the FBI is that this substance may be incorporated into a dirty bomb with devastating consequences over a wide area. The disappearance is publicized by highly conservative talk radio host Dallas Wolf, and FBI agent Nate Foster is sent to work undercover with a small local white-supremacist militia group headed by Vince Sargent in order to gain access to Wolf. The FBI creates a fictitious medical supply company which is concerned with the handling and storage of radioactive material, for Foster's possible use.

The militia members are highly violent, and Foster narrowly stops an attack by them on an interracial couple. However, through Sargent he does manage to get into contact with Wolf by offering him money to support his radio program on the White America Network. In the meantime, Foster gains the confidence of Andrew Blackwell, the head of the Aryan Alliance, a national explicitly Nazi organization, by rescuing him from an attack at a white-supremacy march. Blackwell wants to recruit Foster to his organization, and to show that he's serious about promoting a race war, he shows Foster the map of the whole water-supply system in the District of Columbia.

Members of Sargent's and Blackwell's organizations, and various other white supremacists, attend a party at the home of Gerry Condon, an engineer. Foster spends some time talking with Condon, and learns that he is fully a white supremacist but not a politically active one ("I avoid political stuff – not my thing"). His young daughter even refers to their tree-house as a place of refuge when the "mud people" come. However, Condon holds these parties just so that white supremacists can get together socially, and he actually despises them as being on alcohol and drugs and using coarse language. Condon and his family are highly refined, and even though antisemitic he much appreciates the conductor Leonard Bernstein. He wonders what kind of world children will grow up in, and he mainly is interested in having a whites-only society (rather than in attacking nonwhites), since in his view it was white men who created civilization.

So Foster finally brings $7500 to Wolf, purportedly from an investor who would like to contribute more if Wolf demonstrates his seriousness in promoting a race war. Foster tells Wolf about the Aryan Alliance's possession of the map of the D.C. water-supply system, and indicates that the investor wants information about Wolf's similar practical intentions. It is here that Wolf would presumably describe use of the stolen radioactive material, but instead Wolf returns the $7500 and kicks Foster out of his house. Wolf goes to FBI, reporting what Foster has tried to do, and explains that he is just a public entertainer telling people what they want to hear – he couldn't care less about what he is saying. The FBI's project has collapsed and they shut it down, pointing out that the map of the water-supply system is only what Blackwell shows in order to recruit members, with no practical use.

Foster returns to Conway some white-supremacist books he has borrowed, and gains the complete confidence of Conway in his dedication to the white-supremacist cause. Conway finally recruits Foster to his own project, for through his medical supply "company" Foster has the ability to obtain powerful explosives. Foster works with Conway and two associates, both totally clean-cut, to build a dirty bomb, and the FBI raids their operation and recovers the missing cesium-137.

What is to be learned from this story, which was inspired by real events? First, it doesn't end as might have been expected: the true villains were not the obvious, rabble-rousing hooligans such as our current Proud Boys and Three Percenters, but rather the Gerry Conways: highly cultured, highly rational, leading an exemplary family and social life, but dedicated to creating a whites-only society. Timothy McVeigh, following the 1978 novel **The Turner Diaries** in carrying out the bombing of the federal building in Oklahoma City which killed 168 people, was highly rational in his quest to institute chaos leading to race war.

This is why it is so important to combat Trumpism, to keep it from growing even in the dethronement of its progenitor. (But unfortunately, it seems that Trump is going to be around for a long time, actively building the cause of white supremacy.) Trump's hard-core supporters, numbering perhaps 30% of the electorate, have no qualms about his constant lying, his denigration of the mass media, his attacks on science and rational thinking, his misogyny, his blatant rejection of democratic process, his disregard of the rule of law; they really don't care about anything other than maintaining white supremacy in our country. Many of them will constitute the storm troopers when widespread chaos is spread by the Timothy McVeighs and Gerry Conways. To avoid this fate, it will be vital to build an anti-right front as described in the previous column, and socialists must eschew their previous refusal to have anything to do with the Democratic Party.

Column 9: Terrorism. (draft)

In the last column we reviewed the movie
"Imperium" based on the experiences of undercover
FBI agent Mike German who infiltrated white
supremacist organizations, as related in his book
Thinking Like a Terrorist published in 2008. Here we
shall see how the author approaches the problem of
terrorism, in contradiction to the way that terrorism
had been handled and how in fact it still is being
handled today. He explains that terrorists are not
mental misfits but rather are following a rational
strategy which we don't understand, and he gives ways
of dealing effectively with terrorist groups depending
on the legitimacy of their cause.

German defines terrorist attacks as being "acts
of war against unprotected citizenry." "Terrorism
victimizes an entire nation, an entire population, an
entire culture. It is a crime against humanity."
However, we in the U.S. are unable to see our own
acts as terroristic. "The enemy engages in terrorism;
we engage only in counterterrorism."

"But the groups we consider terrorists don't
regard themselves as terrorists either. … They defend
their actions as morally justifiable, necessary responses
to oppression. …
Terrorists firmly believe they are the persecuted
victims of an evil injustice, and [that] they have the
right to resist their oppression by any means necessary.

This confidence in the righteousness of their cause is what drives terrorist groups to write their manifestos and publish their declarations of war." For terrorists, terrorism is all about the message.

So we're clear that terrorism constitutes heinous attacks on uninvolved civilians (rather than, for example, direct attacks on an occupying army). However, such attacks are carried out by rational human beings, just like us; terrorists are not mentally ill, nor are they people who (to quote a theory propounded by a foremost proponent of the theory that terrorists are primarily driven by psychological factors) have a particular psychological mind-set called "terrorist psycho-logic" that compels them to engage in terrorism. This expert believes that "a great deal has gone wrong in the lives of people who are drawn to terrorism", describing terrorists as "outcasts … from the margins of society", with "personal feelings of inadequacy", who join terrorist groups simply "to belong", to feel "that what they did mattered", and to "heal their inner wounds by attacking the outside enemy".

Gross misunderstanding such as this prevents us from dealing with terrorism in a rational, effective way. Indeed, we do not even understand the strategy of terrorist groups, which is to wage a war of attrition, damaging the economic infrastructure and costing the government to spend huge amounts of money on maintaining security as well as increasingly demonstrating the ineffectiveness and barbarism of the government they are attacking and claiming the mantle of legitimacy of their own cause in the eyes of more and more people. The terrorists are quite aware of the fact that they are weak and the government is strong, and their strategy is to divide the populace into two components, "us" and "them". Governments fall into the trap of furthering this division by waging an indiscriminate "war on terrorism" which flouts its own proclaimed rule of law.

Accordingly, German distinguishes between "legitimately motivated terrorists" (such as the Irish Republican Army which fought against the British occupation of Northern Ireland) and "extremist terrorists" such as the Ku Klux Klan. The terrorist group wages its struggle on behalf of an "identity group" which may or may not actually be oppressed: the Catholics in Northern Ireland in the case of the Irish Republican Army, and all white people in the case of the Ku Klux Klan.

However, being "legitimately motivated" doesn't mean that the terrorist group legitimately represents its identity group or that using violence to redress its grievance is legitimate. "While these groups may claim a legitimate motive, if to achieve those ends they choose illegitimate means – extortion, violence, and other organized criminal activity – they are still terrorists." But recognition by the government of the legitimate grievance does open the road to a negotiated political solution to the insurgency. Nonetheless, the government must strictly maintain control of security, while not using this as a substitute for addressing legitimate grievances.

Regarding "extremist terrorists", the government foremost must maintain its legitimacy by adhering strictly to the rule of law, thereby thwarting the terrorists' strategy of obtaining the aura of legitimacy for themselves. Trying captured terrorists in open court with full rights for the defense and incontrovertible prosecuting evidence makes clear the government's legitimacy. This of course was not true of the FBI's five COINTELPRO programs, targeting the Communist Party (initiated in 1956), the Socialist Workers Party (1961), White Hate (1964), Black Nationalists (1967), and the New Left (1968). Because of the FBI's often immoral and sometimes illegal activities, most evidence gathered during COINTELPRO was ultimately worthless to a criminal prosecution and to mobilizing public approbation. The result was that COINTELPRO techniques were ineffective as well as being harmful to the rule of law – not the right way to deal with terrorism!

Column 10: Fascism. (draft)

In *Thinking Like a Terrorist* published in 2008, Mike German proposes a Government Accountability Scale ranging from fascism to a "free government" (democracy), pointing out that most governments fall somewhere in the middle, between these two extremes. One purpose of making such an evaluation is to determine the legitimacy of terrorist groups' call for self-determination: attacking a fascist government would likely be considered justifiable, but attacking a democratic government would not be legitimate. (This consideration is independent of the particular acts of the terrorist group.)

What concerns us here is understanding the characteristics of fascism, so that we can prevent its rise in a basically democratic country such as ours. But first let us make clear what the features are of the opposite extreme, that of a "free government". German provides the following list:

- Respect for the supremacy of the law
- Free and fair elections
- Freedom of speech and assembly
- Freedom of the press
- Freedom of religion
- Due process of law and an independent judiciary
- Legal protections of minority rights

- The right to a publicly funded education
- The right to private property and free markets
- Civilian control of the military
- Open access to government records
- The freedom to emigrate

Except for the evidently unrestricted free markets, hopefully socialists will strive to fully implement these points. And even regarding capitalism, some socialists (myself included) see the need for a substantial role of small-scale private enterprise for an indefinite period. (Please see my column on Ralph Miliband's practical model of socialism published in June 2020.)

Quoting Robert O. Paxton's *The Anatomy of Fascism* published in 2004, German lists the "mobilizing passions" that drive the political behavior that marks fascist regimes:

- A sense of overwhelming crisis beyond the reach of any traditional solutions
- The primacy of the group, toward which one has duties superior to every right, whether individual or universal, and the subordination of the individual to it
- The belief that one's group is a victim, a sentiment that justifies any action, without legal or moral limits, against its enemies, both internal and external

- Dread of the group's decline under the corrosive effects of individualist liberalism, class conflict, and alien influences
- The need for closer integration of a purer community, by consent if possible, or by exclusionary violence if necessary
- The need for authority by natural chiefs (always male), culminating in a national chieftain who alone is capable of incarnating the group's historical destiny
- The superiority of the leader's instinct over abstract and universal reason
- The beauty of violence and efficacy of will, when they are devoted to the group's success
- The right of the chosen people to dominate others without restraint from any kind of human or divine law, right being decided by the sole criterion of the group's prowess within a Darwinian struggle

Adherence to such passions helps us to identify where persons are on the fascism-democracy scale.

Are die-hard supporters of Trump fascists? There are various ways in which they can be seen as being different from the Nazis of Germany, so many socialists simply dismiss the fear that Trump has been laying the groundwork for fascism in our country. But while all Nazis are fascists, not all fascists are Nazis. As German emphasizes, Nazism is a particular militant, racist, anti-Semitic political philosophy. "Fascism, by contrast, is not an ideology but rather a behavior – a method of securing and exercising political power." The advantage of German's Government Accountability Scale is that it allows people's outlook to be placed in the continuum between outright fascism and full-fledged democracy; the danger is not simply from those who are full-fledged fascists but also – more importantly – from those who are approaching the extreme of fascism. Thus it is the latter group of people whose views we have to combat by vigorously promoting democracy. In this sense the die-hard supporters of Trump indeed are fascists, and we must not be lulled to sleep by the claim that many of them are not Nazi fascists.

Of further interest: In 2019 Mike German published a book *Disrupt, Discredit, and Divide: How the new FBI Damages Democracy*. It shows how FBI leaders exploited the fear of terrorism in the aftermath of 9/11 to shed the legal constraints imposed on them in the 1970s in the wake of Hoover-era civil rights abuses, thereby undermining public confidence in justice and the rule of law.

Column 12: The Danger of Trumpism. (draft)
(An elaboration of this essay is given as Appendix B.)

How dangerous is Trumpism? Are people not more rational, long-term, than this, able to reject much of Trumpism once the Leader is out of power and not setting the agenda? To get insight into such possibilities, we examine what transpired in the Soviet Union with the rise of Stalin.

I have just read **Let History Judge** by Roy Medvedev (1989, Revised and Expanded Edition, Columbia University Press). This book, translated from the Russian, is indeed a weighty tome: 903 pages, three full pounds! In it the author exhaustively analyzes what occurred in the Soviet Union under the domination of Stalin, commencing in the late 1920's and extending to his death in 1953. In doing so he demonstrates the falsity of many interpretations of Stalin's rule: that he continued the building of socialism initiated by the Bolsheviks led by Lenin, that his actions were necessitated by the objective conditions facing the new revolutionary society, that he was a great war-time leader, that he was surrounded by countless intrigues against the socialist society which had to be destroyed by vigorously rooting out "the enemies of the people", etc.

For Stalin was an incomparably brutal despot whose only interest was in safeguarding and expanding his own control of the Soviet state. He held "show trials" at which his political opponents were forced to plead guilty to imaginary conspiracies after being viciously tortured by his secret police and even threatened with retribution against their family members. In this way, by 1938, almost all of the "old Bolshevik" leaders of Lenin's time were killed. He wiped out any communist leaders, at all levels, who might oppose him, even those who had served him loyally. He had huge populations, numbering in the hundreds of thousands, transported to slave labor camps in the harsh hinterland, where many of them died. He wiped out much of the technical and cultural intelligentsia which loyally served the Soviet state. In the years prior to Germany's invasion of Russia in 1941, he also utterly decimated most of the Army command apparatus (from almost all of the generals on down to the lowest levels), thus ensuring Germany's initial battlefield success and the loss of millions of troops through encirclement. The list of Stalin's criminal behavior in thwarting the development of socialism in the Soviet Union could go on and on.

Okay, Stalin was a horribly bad guy, one of the very worst in history, but what has that got to do with us and the struggle against Trumpism? For us what is of particular relevance is the effect which Stalin's rule had on the people of the Soviet Union. First off, the Soviet Communist Party was hegemonic, brooking no opposition while claiming to be ruling as the instrument of working class. It was supposed to be internally democratic, but in reality it was totally top-down, with lower bodies simply implementing directives from above. Even cadres for whom it was obvious that they were being wrongly accused of imaginary crimes would sometimes just plead guilty in order not to impeach the prestige of the Party. (Many others, of course, were forced to plead guilty after enduring severe torture.) This was the quintessence of the one-party state!

At the village level, for example, the head functionary (a Party member, of course) would be given a quota of the number of well-off peasants who were enemies of the state and therefore had to be shipped off to the slave-labor camps, and the functionary readily complied even while realizing that these people had done nothing against the Soviet state. The head of a mining operation, for example, might be told of a vast conspiracy to sabotage output, and he would readily accuse his staff members (most of whom were thereupon shot or given ten-year sentences of hard labor, not long after which the head himself would be arrested and shot). Throughout the country people were making wild false accusations against each other, usually to protect themselves and often to rise economically by taking their places. But through all this carnage the great majority of people, having little information about what was going on except that provided by the Party and believing in the existence of these claimed conspiracies all around themselves, continued to support the government; Stalin was genuinely revered by most at the time of his death!

So let us not be complacent about the danger of Trumpism, thinking that our long history of formal (bourgeois) democracy is going to protect us from the irrationality of people in following Trumpism. It can happen here!

Column 13: The Case for Anti-Communism. (draft)
(This essay is to be published in two parts.)

The following is a two-part series making the case for anti-communism, at least as much as possible given that its practice has been to stifle progressive change in the U.S. and to promote U.S. imperialism throughout the world. Indeed a tough row to hoe, but please bear with me in understanding that there have been valid reasons for adopting anti-communism in one's ideology. If you have no understanding of your apparent enemy's thinking, how can you forthrightly communicate with her/him and possibly turn her/him around?

I was (and still am) a 1960's radical, radicalized by the Vietnam War. In fact, along with 149 other young Americans of draft age, I signed a statement published in the *New York Herald Tribune* in May 1964 stating that "believing that we should not be asked to fight against the people of Vietnam, we herewith state our refusal to do so". This act occurred well before the anti-war movement attained momentum, and it was part of the process which caused me to question my liberal middle-class worldview (as happened with so many youths in the 1960's),

The Vietnam War was a travesty of everything that America supposedly stood for, and it was clear that its (only) justification was anti-communism.

White liberals were gung-ho for the burgeoning civil rights movement at this time, but equally gung-ho for pursuing the war (at least until it turned sour). Even most Black civil-rights leaders supported the war, and Martin Luther King Jr. had to break with them when he opposed the war and stated that "the greatest purveyor of violence in the world today is my own government".

So, with the Vietnam War, the whole edifice of (political) liberalism in the U.S. came crashing down. Many of us war protesters, seeing the malignant role played by anti-communism, became "Marxist-Leninists" (communists) inspired by the victories of the Chinese and Cubans over Western imperialism. Anti-communism was revealed to function as justification for the brutal exploitation of the underdeveloped countries (the "Third World") by our own ruling (economic) class. It was calculatively peddled to the American people by politicians, the mass media, the education system, religious leaders – the whole Establishment – for the benefit of our capitalists. And yet, is it possible that there was also rational justification for anti-communism?

Let us consider the career of Robert Conquest, a well-established historian who was also a staunch anti-communist, serving in his later years as Senior Research Fellow and Scholar-Curator of the East European Collection at the (conservative) Hoover Institute of Stanford University. (He died in 2015 at age 98.) He supported the Reagan military buildup and the Nicaraguan Contras. Most of his political analysis and writings concerned the Soviet Union, especially during the Stalin era. (We shall come to these later.)

Conquest vehemently warned us of the threat posed by the Soviet Union and its "anti-imperialist" followers in the Third World, but let us look at his book **Reflections on a Ravaged Century** (Norton & Company, 2000) at how he considered the actual imperialism which radicalized Americans were reacting to. On pages 251 and 252 he dismisses "anti-imperialism" as well as opposition to "neocolonialism" and to identification of the "American Empire". As mainstream U.S. ideology portrayed, he viewed the United States (aided particularly by the English-speaking economically developed countries of Britain, Canada, Australia, and New Zealand) as leading the world to democracy and economic progress – in short, the notion of American exceptionalism.

How does Conquest fare concerning the Vietnam War, in which the function of anti-communism was starkly revealed to be but a cover for outright imperialism? In his book he devotes only a page (p. 234) to that topic, and spends most of it criticizing McNamara's handling of the war effort, saying that "he undertook a responsibility involving the lives of scores of thousands of Americans and many more Vietnamese". Conquest must be referring to people killed in the war – the body count of Americans was indeed almost three score (58,318, to be exact) – but "many more Vietnamese"?? Estimates of the number of Indochinese killed because of the U.S. effort to subjugate them range up to four million persons. This number is on a par with the millions of people killed in the Soviet Union by the Stalin regime during the 1930's, which Conquest so rightly and usefully exposed, but he betrays no comprehension of the horrific results visited upon the Indochinese peoples by the blind acceptance of anti-communism.

More recently, there was the successful anti-apartheid struggle in South Africa. Militarily, it was aided (by training and supply of weapons) by the Soviet Union and East Germany, while the United States was the last holdout in supporting this noxious system. Conquest has nothing to say about this in his book, even though apartheid was succeeded by the democratically elected government of Nelson Mandela in 1994, six years before publication of his book. And even in the final years of the 1990's, it had become clear that the system of capitalist exploitation tied to Western imperialism would continue to immiserate the masses of Blacks in that country.

So what makes Robert Conquest a candidate for the case of possibly supporting anti-communism? It is that he convincingly exposed the horrors of Stalinist society at a time when many American intellectuals ignored or excused what had gone on in the Soviet

Union in the 1930's. He wrote two immensely
detailed books: **Harvest of Sorrow** (Oxford
University Press, 1986) on the forced collectivization
of agriculture in the early 1930's, focused on the
Ukraine; and **The Great Terror** (1968, Macmillan
Company; updated 1990, Oxford University Press) on
Stalin's purges of 1936-1938 of everyone who might
oppose him. Many millions of Soviet citizens died –
quite unnecessarily – during these times, and
Conquest's reporting and analysis was very thorough
and convincing. (The first book had 1537 references,
while the second had 2339 references.)

In spite of his blinders regarding the deleterious
effects of anti-communism, Robert Conquest deserves
much praise for his historical work exposing the
almost unimaginable monstrosity that was the Soviet
Union under the Stalin dictatorship, and which other
"Marxist-Leninist" advocates of a one-party
dictatorship pretending to rule in the name of the
working class are susceptible to following. As a
staunch anti-communist, he was a highly rational
person, and – one must give him the benefit of the
doubt – greatly concerned about the welfare of human
civilization. On a personal level, I must admit that I
feel closer to Robert Conquest than to socialists who,
while justifiably being reluctant to have anything to do
with the Democratic Party, have not considered it
absolutely imperative to prevent Donald Trump from
remaining in the White House; as the night descends,
many of them chose instead to challenge the

Democratic Party's presidential nominee even in electoral swing states where it might have made the difference.

Column 14: The Art of War (draft)

Time for some ancient Chinese culture! We discuss a famous Chinese book, **The Art of War** by Sun Tzu, which was composed during the fourth century B.C. Why are we interested in a book on the conduct of warfare, especially when we have wars raging all around the planet which we want to put an end to? The reason is that we indeed have much to learn from this book, which emphasizes how to win without actually fighting. My favorite passage is the following:

8. To foresee a victory which the ordinary man can foresee is not the acme of skill;

9. To triumph in battle and be universally acclaimed "Expert" is not the acme of skill, for to lift an autumn down requires no great strength; to distinguish between the sun and moon is no test of vision; to hear the thunderclap is no indication of acute hearing.

Commentary by Chang Yü: By "autumn down" Sun Tzu means rabbits' down, which on the coming of autumn is extremely light.

Footnote: To win a hard-fought battle or to win one by luck is no mark of skill.

10. Anciently those called skilled in war conquered an enemy easily conquered.

Footnote: The enemy was conquered easily because the experts previously had created appropriate conditions.

11. And therefore the victories won by a master of war gain him neither reputation for wisdom nor merit for valor.

> *Commentary by Tu Mu*: A victory gained before the situation has crystallized is one the common man does not comprehend. Thus its author gains no reputation for sagacity. Before he has bloodied his blade the enemy state has already submitted.

> *Commentary by Ho Yen-hsi*: ... When you subdue your enemy without fighting who will pronounce you valorous?

12. For he wins his victories without erring. "Without erring" means that whatever he does ensures his victory; **he conquers an enemy already defeated**.

> *Commentary by Chen Hao*: In planning, never a useless move; in strategy, no step taken in vain.

13. Therefore the skillful commander takes up a position in which he cannot be defeated and misses no opportunity to master his enemy.

14. Thus a victorious army wins its victories before seeking battle; an army destined to defeat fights in the hope of winning.

This is from Sun Tzu, **The Art of War**, Chapter IV: "Dispositions", pp. 86-87; emphasis added.
(Translated by Samuel B. Griffith, Oxford University Press, London, 1963.)

Given that it is necessary at times to "fight" (usually not physically) to achieve necessary aims, is it not better to "win without fighting" as suggested by Sun Tzu? Is it not best to emulate the Master of War: "He conquers an enemy already defeated"?

There are other insights into waging struggle provided by Sun Tzu. One is that victory is won not by overwhelming the enemy through frontal attack, for a solid defensive line can thwart a numerically superior attack. Rather, the key to victory can be an unexpected flank attack made in conjunction with direct engagement of the two armies.

Of particular interest is Sun Tzu's strategy of always leaving an opening for the enemy's retreat, in order to promote his retreating in disarray rather than being forced to fight to the death. He cites the example of a Chinese general whose army was badly outnumbered and on the verge of total defeat; the general thereupon positioned his troops in an area where there was no possibility of retreat, and indeed his army did fight to the death when the attack came and they saved themselves! The lesson that I draw from this outlook is that, in unavoidable conflict, one should not attempt to crush the "enemy", but rather endeavor to reach an accommodation with her/him which respects her/his legitimate interests.

The Art of War provides most interesting, and occasionally quite relevant, reading. There are actually quite a few translations of Sun Tzu's work, and I've read at least five of them. I've quoted from Griffith's early translation, which is highly readable, but subsequent translations incorporating newly found copies (on individual sticks because paper was not then available) of the composition are more accurate.

Column 15: The Ghost of Marxism (draft)
(This essay is to be published in four parts.)

Introduction

In the nineteen century Karl Marx and Friedrich Engels put forward a vision of "scientific socialism" which energized a great many revolutionaries seeking to transcend capitalism. This was based on Marx's detailed analysis of the working of capitalism. According to the theory he developed, the working class would necessarily be increasingly immiserated, the middle strata would lose their independent well-being and become proletarianized, and the whole capitalist system would collapse, leading to a proletarian revolution which would establish (at least in time) a democratic classless society run by, and for the benefit of, the producers themselves.

This vision of the development of society is not exactly what has occurred since the time of Marx and Engels. Capitalism has overcome many major difficulties and remained in full control, and while a successful proletarian revolution did indeed take place in a mostly peasant society (Russia) under the leadership of a vanguard Communist Party, with the pressure of extremely difficult circumstances this party became a brutal one-party dictatorship ("Stalinism") ruling society supposedly in the interest of the working class and the peasantry. This "really existing socialism" served to point the way forward for a great many socialists, at least until this top-down bureaucratic monstrosity collapsed of its own weight around 1990.

However, there remained increasing numbers of socialists inspired by Marxism who considered democracy to be absolutely essential to the liberation of humankind. This has been termed "bottom-up socialism", although we simply call it "socialism" as being the only ethically valid continuation of the pathbreaking work of Marx and Engels; the fundamental differences between the (dominant) Stalinist version of "Marxism-Leninism" and our "socialism" are presented in our essay "Marxist-Leninist 'socialism'" (www.bcmsocialism.org/marxist-leninist-socialism).

Although rooted in the past, Marxists of all stripes have of course developed Marxist theory through practice under current conditions and in the process become relevant to present society. For example, although Marx and Engels gave overwhelming emphasis to the struggle between the proletariat and bourgeoisie (particularly at the point of production), it no longer is deemed acceptable to thereby ignore non-economic struggles ("for appropriate resolution when the working class finally takes over"), a salient example of which was racist opposition to school busing in Boston by some Stalinists in the 1960's in the name of not disturbing working-class unity.

But the ghost of the past, of the errors and current irrelevance in the certain development of

Marxism in both theory and practice, lives on. In some cases we call for fundamental change in the outlook of traditional Marxism, such as now regarding small-scale private enterprise as being essential indefinitely for the new socialist society; in other cases we warn against not fully rejecting wrong ideas and practices, such as vanguardism. Our view is that those Marxists who are fully cognizant of the necessity of democracy in a socialist society are clearly on the right track, and our aim with this essay is to bring to their attention the possible presence of the ghost of Marxism.

"Scientific Socialism"

As outlined above, Marx and Engels advocated what they called "scientific socialism", based on Marx's analysis of the then-current working of capitalism. Of course, any science has to be continually improved upon as more relevant information is obtained and new conditions are taken into account, but did Marx's analysis really lay the basis for understanding present-day capitalism? To what extent can it be considered to inform modern economic theory, so that its product was really "scientific" socialism?

Michio Morishima[1] has tackled this question from a viewpoint sympathetic to Marx's theories, seeking to incorporate them as much as possible into modern economics. In the introduction to his book (p. 5) he writes: "We make Marx stand out not only for his own sake, but against the economic theory of our

time. Our aim is to recognize the greatness of Marx
from the viewpoint of modern advanced economic
theory and, by so doing, to contribute to the
development of our science." Nonetheless, after
exhaustive analysis he finds that Marx's labor theory
of value, his theory of exploitation, and his theory of
the breakdown of the capitalist mode of production are
not generally suitable to current economic science (p.
4).

This is not to say that Marx's insights into the
nature of capitalism are not still of great value to us,
but rather that taken as a whole Marxist economic
theory cannot be taken as fully "scientific", and its
result, "scientific socialism", isn't really that. This
really shouldn't be a problem for us. For example,
according to the labor theory of value, in an eight-hour
day the first five hours of work provide fair
compensation to your employer for what she/he is
paying you for the purchase of your labor-power, but
the product of your remaining three hours is just
grabbed to enrich her/him. This is a seemingly
scientific explanation of "exploitation" of the working
class, and it can energize socialist revolutionaries. But
does such a calculation really matter to ordinary
workers? They know the boss is screwing them in any
case, and that it would be better for themselves to have
all of the fruits of their labor.

I should point out that the early Marxists
(especially Engels) attempted to systematize
materialist dialectics as the basis for a scientific
understanding of the development of society, just as

advanced mathematics provides such a basis for the science of physics. A dialectical outlook, of everything being in a state of flux rather than qualitatively fixed (as promoted by bourgeois ideology), can be of great help in such understanding, especially since there are definite laws of dialectical development to provide guidance. However, I am grieved that so few socialist activists today take the study of dialectics seriously. I have attempted to incorporate feminist theory into the traditional Marxist presentation of the theory of dialectical materialism[2], and as well have demonstrated that Engels and others were dead wrong in viewing non-living phenomena (such as described by physics and chemistry) as exhibiting dialectical development[3].

The danger: If one regards traditional Marxism as having laid the basis for a valid "scientific socialism", one may tend not to try to develop an accurate understanding of what is going on in the world; after all, the "science of society" has already been worked out and all that is really necessary is to apply it to current conditions. The result can be unquestioning dogmatism.

Workerism

As described in the Introduction section, Marx and Engels viewed the transition to socialism (and subsequently to the communist classless society) as resulting from a proletarian revolution following the inevitable collapse of capitalism. Thus what was primary in this scenario was the fundamental conflict between the proletariat and the bourgeoisie, particularly at the point of production. That the working class could, and indeed must be, the instrument for the attainment of a new, humanly decent society was certainly reasonable, for that class alone could successfully challenge the economic rule of the capitalists, and they would be stirred to such action through their collective experience in production. And such potential for class action was well demonstrated by the Bolshevik revolution in Russia in 1917, which was meant to spark proletarian revolution throughout Europe.

Unfortunately, the working class did not successfully rise up as required in central and western Europe in the aftermath of World War I; these workers were too accepting of the capitalist ordering of industrial society in spite of the hardships of the war. We cannot rightfully blame the willingness of each country's working class to fight for their country against the workers of other countries, on a "labor aristocracy" misleading them. The problem was far deeper: the working class simply wasn't doing what Marxists wanted and expected them to do. And now in the United States we find Donald Trump with the fervent support of a very large section of the working class in laying the groundwork for an authoritarian, and possibly fascist, society.

We have to stop kidding ourselves, in our great overemphasis on the working class as the instrument of effecting socialism. Yes, certainly the working class is still key to this transition, because of its numerical size, its vital role in the production process, and its collective experience. But workers are not one-dimensional, as many Marxists tend to believe. There are many non-economic struggles which are vitally important in shaping workers' lives and ideology (for better or worse), concerning such matters as racism, homophobia, reproductive rights, misogyny, spirituality and religion, environmental degradation, family, poverty, even animal rights, etc. At any given time, one or another of these non-economic struggles may be primary for people, rather than that against capitalist exploitation. (Right now in the U.S., there is the powerful Black Lives Matter movement which envelopes the attention both of Blacks and of many white people and other people of color.)

So socialist activists must immerse themselves in both economic and non-economic struggles for progressive social change. Rather than treating middle-class people merely as auxiliaries in the struggle for socialism, they must accept them as equal participants in this struggle and work integrally with them on common progressive goals. In all of this political work with both working-class and middle-class people, socialist activists must advocate their vision of the new society as appropriate, without trying to dominate progressive organizations "for the sake of the revolution".

The danger: There may be gross overemphasis on the role of the working class in effecting socialism, with attendant negligence in participating in non-economic struggles and belittling of the vital role of middle-class activists in these struggles.

Vanguardism

The extreme version of vanguardism, of course, is that of the practice of the Stalinist version of Marxism-Leninism and of the communist parties around the world which followed in its footsteps. In this outlook, the communist party rules society on behalf of the people as a whole, but it itself solely determines what is to be done; the rest of society just follows the esteemed judgment of its leaders. And even within the "vanguard party", although in principle all party members have the right to debate and help set policy to be followed, in practice the higher levels dictate to the lower levels what is to be done. Forming factions within the party advocating a political course of action is forbidden. This "dictatorship of the proletariat" is actually the dictatorship of a small group of top-level all-wise people.

So "vanguardism" refers to the attitude that you, because of your superior knowledge and ability, are able to determine what others are to do, politically. It is inimical to democracy, of course, and thus to socialism as we envision it. Trotskyism, the other major version of Marxism-Leninism, often makes a serious effort to function democratically within the party, such as by expressly allowing the existence of factions; this is hardly surprising, considering how undemocratically they have been treated by Stalinists.

But even well-meaning Trotskyist organizations may, in my opinion, succumb at least partially to vanguardism. As a case in point, in Seattle we have on the City Council Kshama Sawant, a member of the Trotskyist party Socialist Alternative. She has been doing an outstanding job and is now in her third term of office. Socialist Alternative may be considered to be a vanguard party, to which I have no objection so long as it is meant to be *a* vanguard party rather than *the* (sole) vanguard party. This means that members are expected to carry out decisions arrived at by the party's leadership, although the leadership is to be selected periodically through a democratic process involving all the membership. In principle I have no objection to such functioning in order to ensure that the party carries out a chosen political line (although I don't think that doing this strictly is very useful), but she was ordered by her party's leadership concerning how to conduct her political work: how she should vote on a controversial appointment for the police chief, and who should be or not be in her office staff. I feel that office-holders should be free to make such decisions themselves (while giving serious consideration to the advice of the party), in order to be able to respond properly to the concerns of their constituents.

So, in contrast to an attitude of vanguardism, we must have complete democracy (again, "socialism from below"). This means in particular one-person/one-vote (rather than one-dollar/one-vote), the right and ability of the people to vote a socialist government out of office, the rule of law (an independent judiciary and a constitution). The middle class must be expected to have a major say in the shaping of the new society, and in fact small-scale private enterprise must be regarded as existing indefinitely in the new socialist society. (This outlook of continued forms of capitalism constitutes a fundamental break with traditional Marxism, and is explained in detail by Miliband[4].) Our outlook must be the self-organization of people, rather than expecting them to just implement policies arrived at from above.

The danger: It is easy to lapse into a vanguardist attitude, even while rejecting the extreme authoritarianism of Stalinism. The antidote to vanguardism is complete reliance on democratic functioning, and resisting the urge to dominate.

REFERENCES

1. Michio Morishima, **Marx's Economics: A Dual Theory of Value and Growth** (Cambridge University Press, 1973).

2. Dave Jette, **A Reformulation of Dialectical Materialism** (self-published, available at www.lulu.com; 2019). A brief version of this work is given in **Beyond Classical Marxism** (self-published, available at www.lulu.com, 2020), as its Chapter 2, as well as at www.bcmsocialism.org/dialectical-materialism.

3. Dave Jette, appendix "Is Nature Dialectical" of **A Reformulation of Dialectical Materialism** (self-

published, available at www.lulu.com; 2019). It is
also available at www.bcmsocialism.org/is-nature-
dialectical/.

4. Ralph Miliband, **Socialism for a Sceptical Age**
(Version, 1994). A synopsis of this economic model is
given in **Beyond Classical Marxism** (self-published,
available at www.lulu.com, 2020), as Section A of its
Chapter 5, as well as at
www.bcmsocialism.org/socialist-economy/.

Published in January 2021 by Organizing Upgrade at https://organizingupgrade.com/socialists-tasks-in-an-anti-right-front-response-to-calvin-cheung-miaw/

Socialists' Tasks in an Anti-Right Front: Reply to Calvin Cheung-Miaw

By Dave Jette

Trump is out, and Biden is in. Where do we go from here in combatting the cancer of Trumpism and working toward the transformation of our society in a socialist direction? Calvin Cheung-Miaw's piece on Organizing Upgrade, "The Pivot of U.S. Politics: Racial Justice and Democracy," stresses how intertwined the struggles for racial justice and democracy necessarily are. Furthermore, it offers a provocative proposal: to build and keep together an anti-right front in order to combat the long-term grave danger of Trumpism. There are, however, two weaknesses in the article which need to be addressed more fully if this strategy is going to gain traction: one is fuller elaboration of how deep the threat of fascism is, and the other is not giving enough weight to the development of a large and united group of progressives and socialists to carry out such an ambitious strategy.

DON'T UNDERESTMATE THE DANGER

The ongoing danger of Trumpism cannot be underestimated. Since Election Day Trump has been claiming, without presenting any sort of proof, that the election was rigged, that he actually won hands down. A poll taken in November found that 77% of Republicans agree with him that the election was fraudulent: mindless people who follow *der führer* wherever he may lead them in safeguarding white supremacy, and unfortunately a very substantial portion of the white working class! Perhaps 30% of the electorate are hard-right followers of Trump, accepting his outrageously blatant lies and his rejection of democracy and the rule of law. Presently they constitute a reserve force for the capitalists, to be used when society further crumbles as neoliberalism tanks. How possible is a transition to an outright authoritarian political system, or even to fascism?

Let us look at the example of Hitler's rise to power in Germany in 1933, with the aid of the collection of essays **Radical Perspectives on the Rise of Fascism in Germany, 1919-1945** (Monthly Review Press, 1989). In the aftermath of World War I, a democratic parliamentary political system was set up in defeated Germany, as the "Weimar Republic." The capitalists were divided into three major factions: heavy industry (iron, steel, mining) focused on domestic economic development; export industry (dynamic, technologically more advanced, and more prosperous) led by machine, electric, and chemical industries as

well as textiles and commercial interests; and
agriculture (the landed aristocracy, particularly the
"Junkers" of Prussia). The "middle class" consisted of
shopkeepers, commodity producers, and salaried
employees, as well as the peasantry. The working
class had strong labor unions and a strong political
party (the Social Democratic Party of Germany, or
"SPD") and a German Communist Party ("KPD")
which had been greatly weakened by the abortive
revolutionary uprisings following World War I.

At first the export-industry fraction of the bourgeoisie
was dominant in representing capital, and the labor
unions and SPD were able to work with this fraction
until 1930 to considerably improve workers'
lives. They were, in fact, so successful that heavy
industry was unable to make a strong profit and the
economic system was in major distress. Therefore
when heavy industry achieved hegemony within the
bourgeoisie over the export industry in the early 1930s,
this fraction refused to collaborate politically with
workers' organizations. At this point the political
system was so dysfunctional that the Weimar
parliament lost most mass support in spite of efforts by
heavy industry to revive it. The only really strong
political parties in the early 1930s were the fascist
NSDAP (the National Socialist German Workers Party
of Hitler, based most strongly in the "middle class")
and the SPD (with some help from the KPD, although
at this time the communists were denouncing the
social democrats as being the main enemy of the
revolution). The capitalists tried to use the NSDAP as
a junior partner in parliament, as a substitute for their

lack of mass following. But Hitler refused any deal other than one making him chancellor, and the capitalists finally capitulated, especially since the NSDAP in the most recent election appeared to be in decline and there was the danger that it would fade away.

So on January 30, 1933 Hitler was appointed chancellor of Germany. He quickly destroyed the labor unions and soon all other political parties, using as necessary the huge army of streetfighters (the SA, or "stormtroopers") which the NSDAP had built up. Through a referendum he had himself and his party declared the sole ruler of Germany, and by 1938 he had replaced the old state bureaucracy with his own followers. Anti-Semitism was eagerly implemented, with Jews deprived of any political or social influence and even of their livelihoods; this treatment was but a prelude to the Holocaust which the Germans carried out in Eastern Europe as soon as they were able to, when Germany invaded Poland in September 1939.

This transformation could occur in Germany because, unlike in the U.S. now, the various fractions of the bourgeoisie had lost most mass support in the parliament. But what will happen as capitalist neoliberalism unrelentingly sinks the living conditions of the masses of Americans? The groundwork has been laid for the advent of a highly authoritarian society, even for fascism: the campaign to discredit the election and build a fascist tendency has put in place key pieces for a demagogue far more skilled than Trump to ride this current to power in 2024. And the depth of racism in our country is driving this frenzy on the right. It is not possible to understand the irrationality of the Trumpists without taking this racism into account, just as the idea of Aryan supremacy ("the master race") taking hold in Germany undergirded so much of what seems today to have been so irrational as well as murderous. The Jan. 6 insurrection at the Capitol by a mob displaying Confederate and neo-Nazi regalia should strip away any lingering denial on this point.

A TALL ORDER

The Cheung-Miaw essay recognizes this great danger, and proposes the creation of an Anti-Right Front which includes not only progressives and socialists, but also moderate Democrats and even moderate Republicans who are willing to risk their political careers in order to combat the slide to Trumpism. The essay acknowledges that since racial justice issues tend to divide the anti-right front, "it will require some finesse to keep an anti-right front together under a Biden administration, but backing away from racial justice struggles will only weaken our long-term capacity to fight the forces pushing white minority rule." Thus the essay is advocating a sea-change in the way that socialists view the two-party system: the current outlook on the two-party system held by so many socialists, that we should have nothing to do with the Democratic Party (for very good reasons, of course!) is simply obsolete and counterproductive.

But an Anti-Right "Front"? This is certainly a tall order, and socialists can hardly expect to pull it off themselves. For the time being it must be informal, but still being engendered by our active participation in struggles for racial justice and democracy, linking them together (ideologically) as much as possible. It may eventually be useful to form an organization – at first basically a listserv for exchange of information and strategy – of progressives and socialists who are committed to this long-term project of building an anti-right front as expounded in this article, with emphasis on the struggle for racial justice as being essential to achieving democratic functioning. It is critical that those progressives and socialists who do agree with the anti-right front strategy continue and deepen their communications, strategize together, and put other differences in proportion to the urgency of stopping fascism. Already we have the unfortunate example of the Democratic Socialists of America, the largest socialist group in the United States today, refusing to support Biden in order to combat the grave threat of Trumpism; socialists are simply going to have to give up their rigorous antipathy to having anything to do with the Democratic Party, if we are to survive.

APPENDIX B: **Elaboration of "Looking Forward" Column 12: The Danger of Trumpism**
(unpublished)

Now that Donald Trump has been prevented from continuing in office, are we out of the woods of "Trumpism"? Or has the battle just begun? How should we relate to the Biden administration, in order to ensure that Trumpism will not raise its ugly head effectively again?

To answer such questions, we must realize that Trumpism is not simply a highly conservative reaction to our society's current problems. The fact is that Trump has released the genie from the bottle, liberating the worst of what is America. It is not simply that he has based his political appeal explicitly on white supremacy, which the Republican Party has long championed in a veiled way (the "Southern strategy" of Richard Nixon). Trump has actively promoted misogyny; blatant, outright lying by the Leader; flouting of the rule of law, particularly of the Constitution; dismissal as "fake news" any established facts which contradict what one wants to be true; blanket antagonism towards the mass media, as "the enemy of the people"; total distrust of science and the scientific method; public demonstrations of armed, far-right-wing "patriots" in support of his policies; verbal and legal attacks on "The Other", in this case immigrants of color and Moslems; expression of utter contempt for persons who oppose or disagree with him. Evidently at least 30% of Americans are hardcore, wholeheartedly supporting all these manifestations of "Trumpism".

But how dangerous is this current infatuation with Trump? Are people not more rational, long-term, than this, able to reject much of Trumpism once the Leader is out of power and not setting the agenda? To get insight into such possibilities, we examine what transpired in the Soviet Union with the rise of Stalin.

I have just read **Let History Judge** by Roy Medvedev (1989, Revised and Expanded Edition, Columbia University Press). This book, translated from the Russian, is indeed a weighty tome: 903 pages, three full pounds! In it the author exhaustively analyzes what occurred in the Soviet Union under the domination of Stalin, commencing in the late 1920's and extending to his death in 1953. In doing so he demonstrates the falsity of many interpretations of Stalin's rule: that he continued the building of socialism initiated by the Bolsheviks led by Lenin, that his actions were necessitated by the objective conditions facing the new revolutionary society, that he was a great war-time leader, that he was surrounded by countless intrigues against the socialist society which had to be destroyed by vigorously rooting out "the enemies of the people", etc.

For Stalin was an incomparably brutal despot whose only interest was in safeguarding and expanding his own control of the Soviet state. He held "show trials" at which his political opponents were forced to plead guilty to imaginary conspiracies after being viciously tortured by his secret police and even threatened with retribution against their family members. In this way, by 1938, almost all of the "old Bolshevik" leaders of Lenin's time were killed. He wiped out any communist leaders, at all levels, who might oppose him, even those who had served him loyally. He had huge populations, numbering in the hundreds of thousands, transported to slave labor camps in the harsh hinterland, where many of them died. He wiped out much of the technical and cultural intelligentsia which loyally served the Soviet state. In the years prior to Germany's invasion of Russia in 1941, he also utterly decimated most of the Army command apparatus (from almost all of the generals on down to the lowest levels), thus ensuring Germany's initial battlefield success and the loss of millions of troops through encirclement. The list of Stalin's criminal behavior in thwarting the development of socialism in the Soviet Union could go on and on.

Okay, Stalin was a horribly bad guy, one of the very worst in history, but what has that got to do with us and the struggle against Trumpism? For us what is of particular relevance is the effect which Stalin's rule had on the people of the Soviet Union. First off, the Soviet Communist Party was hegemonic, brooking no opposition while claiming to be ruling as the instrument of working class. It was supposed to be internally democratic, but in reality it was totally top-down, with lower bodies simply implementing directives from above. Even cadres for whom it was obvious that they were being wrongly accused of imaginary crimes would sometimes just plead guilty in order not to impeach the prestige of the Party. (Many others, of course, were forced to plead guilty after enduring severe torture.) This was the quintessence of the one-party state!

At the village level, for example, the head functionary (a Party member, of course) would be given a quota of the number of well-off peasants who were enemies of the state and therefore had to be shipped off to the slave-labor camps, and the functionary readily complied even while realizing that these people had done nothing against the Soviet state. The head of a mining operation, for example, might be told of a vast conspiracy to sabotage output, and he would readily accuse his staff members (most of whom were thereupon shot or given ten-year sentences of hard labor, not long after which the head himself would be arrested and shot). Throughout the country people were making wild false accusations against each other, usually to protect themselves and often to rise economically by taking their places. But through all this carnage the great majority of people, having little information about what was going on except that provided by the Party and believing in the existence of these claimed conspiracies all around themselves, continued to support the government; Stalin was genuinely revered by most at the time of his death!

How could this have happened in a country which had gone through a revolution to transform society into one based on goals of equality and humanity? Well, thanks to Medvedev's highly detailed analysis we know how Stalin was able to subvert the revolution to become his complete tool, how all opposition to his rule was systematically crushed, how an attendant bureaucracy naturally arose, etc. Nonetheless, the lesson to be learned is how frail humankind's best instincts can be, how under certain conditions the worst of our character can rise to the fore and overwhelm all that is civilized. Of course this is what happened in Nazi Germany, and it is the fate that we are faced with, in Trumpism. So let us disregard all complacency and realize that a life-and-death struggle with Trumpism lies before us. This struggle will be all the more necessary as neo-liberal capitalism collapses and the 1% look to an authoritarian government to safeguard their riches.

This struggle against Trumpism must involve, first and foremost, taking part in progressive mass struggles to improve people's lives, for that is how we build the movement for progressive social change. The electoral arena, which usually plays a secondary role in this process (except right now when getting rid of Trump himself is of critical concern), can also be of great use in effecting (limited) progressive reforms such as Medicare for All, and in fostering an overall progressive outlook on goals for the future. I have previously advocated not trying to build an independent progressive party to take on the Democrats (https://bcmsocialism.org/a-new-progessive-party/), but instead to *use* the two-party system by running unabashedly progressive candidates in Democratic Party primary elections. (After presumably losing the primary, our candidate should no longer be criticizing the successful Democrat, and may even support her/his campaign if she/he isn't clearly reactionary.) The key is that we must always put forward, in mass struggles and in electoral work, unreservedly progressive politics rather than watering down our politics for the sake of an illusory unity. Especially, we must expose the Biden administration as having nothing to do with the creation of a humane society, and forthrightly call for the replacement of capitalism with socialism.

APPENDIX C: The Partisan Experience

This is the 1970-1973 tale of a New Left organization in Vancouver, Canada which finally committed hari-kari by joining the Communist Party of Canada (Marxist-Leninist. I joined it in late 1971 and quickly rose to membership in its Central Committee. There were other factors accelerating the Partisan Organization's demise, include the need of its top leadership (not including me) to avoid being replaced because of major organizational errors. I published a lengthy analysis of the experience of the Partisan Organization in Theoretical Review #13 (November-December 1979) of the Tucson Marxist-Leninist Collective, and this article is given here. The original draft of this paper was much longer, with an introduction to the political situation in Canada and twenty endnotes, and it is available from the author at dave@jettes.org.

Partisan as a New Left organization

Partisan arose from a New Left organization called the Vancouver Liberation Front (VLF). An excerpt from a document produced during a major internal struggle (in December, 1971, while the organization was still New Left) makes clear that the VLF had no ideological origin in Marxism-Leninism:

The Vancouver Liberation Front was formed in the spring of 1970. The impetus came from a group of student radicals disaffected with the fruitless struggle

The crunch for the VLF came during the
October 1970 crisis, when the bourgeoisie used the
pretext of a political kidnapping and execution by the
Front de Libération de Québec (FLQ) to send the army
to occupy Québec to suppress what they called an
"apprehended insurrection". In Vancouver, the VLF
called a demonstration to support the FLQ. A
thousand people showed up, but the VLF was exposed
as having "nothing to offer in terms of real
organization, or real plans, not even real ideas. The
people went home, dissatisfied and cynical". And the
VLF withdrew from political practice in order to
struggle through a strategy.

In April 1971, after months of internal struggle,
the VLF became the Partisan Party, now with a full-

blown strategy for anti-imperialist revolution based on mobilizing the dispossessed, and with lip service to the socialism of Marx, Lenin, and Mao. They in fact adopted much of their strategy from the Black Panther Party in the U.S., particularly from Eldridge Cleaver concerning the role of the dispossessed and from Huey Newton concerning intercommunalism. (Intercommunalism, a world-view which is supposedly an extension of Lenin's theory of imperialism, differs from Marxism-Leninism in stating that no nation can exist which is not also politically independent, and that the withering away of the state predicted by Marx and Engels is already occurring under capitalism. The first issue of their newspaper, *The Partisan*, after mentioning with approval the burning down of a school in a suburb of Vancouver, laid out the lumpenproletariat-based strategy of the newly-formed Partisan Party:

We all have the same enemy. We share a common oppression as a class of dispossessed people. We are poor and we want our freedom. So far the pigs have kept us divided and ignorant of each other so they can take us on one by one.

What is needed is organization, leadership and strategy. WE HAVE TO DEVELOP TACTICS OF RESISTANCE THAT LET US CHOOSE OUR OWN LOCATIONS AND METHODS OF FIGHTING. We shouldn't become a set-up for the pigs.

In fact, the VLF had turned from adventurism to reformism, implementing a strategy of attaining community-control of everything as a means of securing bases for launching a people's war, *à la* the Chinese and Vietnamese revolutions. Their statement of principles, "What We Want …What We Believe", published in every issue of *The Partisan*, called for direct community control of the means of production, of housing and land, of health centers, of the educational system, and of "people's courts" to judge crimes against the community. While these New Left revolutionaries had adopted a strategy which was objectively reformist, they at least had managed to disabuse themselves of adventurism, as their reply to the terrorist Red Morning Collective in Toronto demonstrates:

The most important factor in any people's war is not the mere military strength of the army, but the political strength of the people. The key factor at any stage of the struggle is the relationship between the vanguard and the people. The struggle is one between the people and the system. To have an armed force substitute itself for one which arises from the struggle in the community is to actively discourage the formation and growth of a true people's army.

The first issue of *The Partisan* was only a one-page wall sheet whose main purpose was to announce the formation of the Partisan Party, but the next ten issues, through November 12, 1971, we substantial, typically running 24 pages and coming out every three weeks. By November the newspaper was being sold at some 60 bookstores, grocery stores, and other community businesses, mostly in Vancouver but also in Victoria, Toronto, Montréal, and even Seattle.

But the Partisans were still New Left revolutionaries, and in the almost complete absence of Marxist-Leninist theory they were just playing at revolution. An example of their naïveté is provided by the following gems from their "People's Vocabulary":

EXPLOITATION – is taking from the poor and giving to the rich.

CAPITALISM – is the poor getting poorer and the rich getting richer.

IMPERIALISM – the capitalists get richer and the world gets poorer.

SOCIALISM – is everybody sharing. A system based on human need, not human exploitation.

In the second half of 1971, the Partisan Party carried out a number of concrete projects within the community. It opened a Community Survival Center as "a place where we can teach and learn from each other through films, classes and rapping, a place out of which we can organize together around the problems in our local areas". Unfortunately, the Center was located in a neighborhood of ethnic Chinese, with whom the Partisans had absolutely no contact, so it never did turn into a community drop-in center. However, out of the Survival Center the Partisans did run a "People's Patrol" to keep the police in line: "Armed with our knowledge of legal rights,

with medical equipment, cameras, and a copy of the
Criminal Code, we have been cruising the city,
stopping at any sign of harassment to advise people of
their rights and to aid them in enforcing those rights."

The Partisan Party did end the year with a
concrete service to the community: a two-day
Christmas party which gave some 1800 people turkey
dinners provided mainly by money demanded from
unions, small businesses, department stores, and
supermarket chains, and which entertained many
children both afternoons. But by then the Partisan
Party was just in the process of recovering from a
major split, the usual fate of New Left revolutionary
organizations shackled with a non-Marxist-Leninist
political line. With the defections, the old leadership
of the Partisan Party was able to recreate the
organization essentially unchallenged, first continuing
the old pre-people's war/community organizing
strategy, but eventually steering the Partisan to
Marxism-Leninism.

The transformation of Partisan into a Marxist-Leninist organization

At the beginning of 1972 the Partisan Party was
recreated; those who had left the previous November
were replaced by a number of new members recruited
during the Christmas Party campaign, and the
organization was ready to start work anew. The top
leadership was strong and effectively unchallenged,
not because they were putting forward correct political
lines to move the organization forward, but because

the theoretical level of the whole organization was
abysmally low. In this situation, with its previous
opposition no longer around, leadership could have
transformed the organization's line into practically
anything. What happened, in fact, was that leadership
came to grasp Marxism-Leninism and brought about
the transformation of the Partisan Party to a Marxist-
Leninist organization. And it is this transformation of
Partisan which makes the story worth telling. The
transformation was carried out from the top, which
was the only way possible in this situation, but the
theoretical level of most of the membership remained
very low, a contradiction which two months later was
to cause the self-destruction of the new Marxist-
Leninist organization, at a time when leadership was
playing a politically reactionary and manipulative role.

Two leaders of Partisan played key roles in the
transformation and destruction of the organization in
1972: Richard Rathwell and David Paterson. Since
the fall of 1971 Paterson was based in Toronto,
working to build up a branch of Partisan in the
East. In Vancouver, Partisan was completely
dominated by Rathwell; even when the Central
Committee in Vancouver was expanded from two to
six members in June, it remained compliant to its head,
Rathwell. It was Paterson in Toronto, supported by
Rathwell and the rest of the Central Committee, who
gave the political leadership which brought about the
transformation of Partisan during the summer. And it
was Rathwell, powerfully aided by the rest of the
Central Committee in Vancouver but behind
Paterson's back, who two months later manipulated

the Partisan Organization into joining *en masse* the Communist Party of Canada (Marxist-Leninist), a revisionist organization of agent-provocateurs.

Starting afresh in 1972, the Partisan Party was still saddled with its strategy of gaining control of the communities for use as base areas in a protracted people's war to overthrow capitalism.

Through discussion with comrades in Québec, however, Paterson was able to see the error of this pre-people's war strategy, and to convince the rest of the Central Committee of the strategic importance of workplace organizing and that the Revolution would take the form of an insurrection in the cities rather than a protracted people's war. At this time the leadership also realized that the approximately twenty members of Partisan did not yet constitute a vanguard party, and "Partisan Party" became "Partisan Organization".

The new political line of Partisan filtered down through the organization only slowly, and the March issue of *The Partisan*, had to be scrapped after printing because it was still promoting the old line. (*The Partisan* was in fact never printed again, mainly because the organization's line was changing so rapidly.)

Externally, Partisan political work pretty well disintegrated in conjunction with the internal turmoil. The People's Patrol never survived the split of the previous November. The Community Survival Center was scheduled to be reopened at a more suitable location, but it fell victim to the change in political line. (Along with it fell a planned Free Breakfast Program, modeled after the Black Panthers'.) On the other hand, the new emphasis on point-of-production organizing resulted in the sponsorship of a series of "Maynights" just after May Day, for the purposes of education, building fraternalism, and recruitment. The three evenings featured films and speakers on working-class struggle, anti-imperialist struggles, and resistance to the state, and led to the recruitment of several workers.

The Partisan political line was in the process of changing, but it was still quite a mess. On May 29th Paterson, now working closely in Toronto with several dropouts from the terrorist organization Red Morning, wrote a demolishing critique of the Black Panther's theory of intercommunalism. In early June, Rathwell brought out a 37-page draft of a strategy paper, "Building a Revolutionary Party of a New Type", and, recognizing the importance of participation in the application of theory to the organization's political line, he tripled the size of the Central Committee in Vancouver, to six. (The only other member was Paterson, in Toronto.) The "Party of a New Type" paper attempted to base itself on Marxism-Leninism and constituted a major break with the old political line, but it was seriously flawed. It remained for Paterson to demonstrate its errors, initially with a criticism of its military strategy which was responded to in a vicious sectarian by one member of the Central Committee, and finally with a 38-page letter (July 9th) giving an overall criticism and of the Central Committee's method of struggle.

Paterson's criticisms were analyzed in great detail, both by the Central Committee and by the membership as a whole. The Central Committee responded by scrapping the "Party of a New Type" paper and drafting a set of Marxist-Leninist principles, the "Statement of Direction", to transform the organization into a Marxist-Leninist one and to guide its future work. Thee were strong objections to the Central Committee's giving theoretical leadership in this struggle, because of its previous sectarian response to Paterson's criticisms. [Members of one section temporarily prevented their head (himself a member of the Central Committee) from arguing the positions coming out of the Central Committee.] But the Central Committee did succeed in leading struggle through the organization over political line. During Paterson's visit to Vancouver in the middle of August, two plenary sessions of the Partisan Organization were held. The "Statement of Direction" was adopted in final form on August 20th, and a new course was set for the organization, under the same leadership. The direction of practical work was entrusted to a Secretariat reporting to the Central Committee, so that the latter body would be able to devote full-time to working out the strategic direction of the organization. Partisan now numbered approximately 25, and it at last seemed destined to provide effective leadership to the new Marxist-Leninist movement in Canada.

But the transformation of the Partisans to Marxist-Leninists was more in form than in content. There was now a set of Marxist-Leninist principles guiding Partisan work, but no real understanding of these principles throughout the organization. During the summer, the struggle over Partisan political line was carried out in a fully collective manner, first in sections each under the leadership of a Central Committee member, and, then, after summation of the struggle by the Central Committee, in a plenary. The Central Committee was in fact putting forward good politics at this time, but cadre, having generally very weak theoretical background, were simply not in a position to evaluate the new political positions coming down – they accepted these positions because they sounded reasonable and were invoked on the authority of the Russian and Chinese revolutions.

Nor was the Central Committee in Vancouver a font of Marxist-Leninist knowledge. As indicated by its initial enthusiastic acceptance of Rathwell's "Party of a New Type" paper, the Central Committee itself hardly knew what it was doing. It did, however, have ready access to classical Marxist-Leninist works, and from these it was able to work up quite a respectable "Statement of Direction". In retrospect one can find many omissions and inaccuracies in the "Statement Direction"; for example, the relationship between the Communist Party (or the pre-Party formation) and the proletariat was hardly touched upon, and there were several references to "testing strategy in practice" (still, the old empiricist attitude that correct strategy derives from direct experience, rather than through the application of political theory to the concrete conditions encountered). But the Central Committee in Vancouver was, after all, just picking out goodies from tis newly-discovered candy store, Marxism-Leninism; it had no solid knowledge of Marxist-Leninist organization, but this transformation was yet to be effected in a real sense.

The liquidation of Partisan

At the beginning of September 1972 the Partisan Organization was finally on the right course, but both its leadership and the rest of its membership were at a very low theoretical level. Paterson, in a letter of July 3rd, had already pointed out the problem:

A high priority must be placed on the development of revolutionary theory. This means we should be reading and studying both historical works and classics of Marxism-Leninism. I would suggest, perhaps, weekly study sessions on different books required of cadre and open to outsiders. The books should be read by everyone and the education prepared by a different person each week. We are far too weak in our knowledge of Marxist-Leninist theory and this must be rectified.

What was actually necessary to do at this point was to liquidate external practice (or rather, not to reinstitute it, for because of the struggle over political line very little of it had been done for months), and to spend several months in systematic study to raise the desperately low theoretical level of everyone. Indeed, the "Statement of Direction" had called for the drawing up of a political program through analysis of the classes and struggles of Canadian society, and struggle over this program would have provided a good counterpoint to the theoretical study. But to Partisan, liquidation of practice was blasphemy. Theory had done its job in providing the "Statement of Direction", and now that the organization was on the right track, it was necessary to make up for lost time and get the Revolution rolling again. Petit-bourgeois haste, practice fetishism, and contempt for theory prevented Partisan from taking the steps necessary to transform itself into a real Marxist-Leninist organization.

What happened instead was that Partisan, in its innocence, was swallowed up by the Communist Party of Canada (Marxist-Leninist), aided by Rathwell and several other not-so-innocent members [*added note: including the present author*] of the Partisan Central Committee. CPC(M-L) had already requested with Partisan "open discussion and debates on various questions facing the people", and on August 14th the Partisan Central Committee had decided to prepare an overview of CPC(M-L)'s political line in order to facilitate such struggle. Such a criticism was never prepared, but the Central Committee did move the organization closer and closer to CPC(M-L). On September 29th, CPC(M-L) asked the Partisan Organization to run its own candidate in the federal election several weeks hence, to accompany its fifty candidates through the country, and the Partisan

Central Committee quickly mobilized the whole organization to this purpose.

The federal election took place, as scheduled. The Partisan candidate lost, pulling in around 150 votes, but a great deal of camaraderie was built up between the Partisans and the members of the Vancouver Branch of CPC(M-L). The Partisans had distributed a large amount of their campaign literature, and they felt ecstatic finally to be doing something on a mass basis to advance the Revolution. On October 21st the Partisan Central Committee (excepting Paterson, of course, who was safely back in Toronto) held a second meeting with Hardial Bains, one of the national leaders of CPC(M-L), who proposed that the Partisan Organization and the Vancouver Branch of CPC(M-L) unite organizationally to form a "Marxist-Leninist Centre of a New Type" in Vancouver. (How a national vanguard Communist Party could place one of its own branches under the discipline of another organization was a question which apparently never occurred to the Partisan leadership.) Bains stated that this Vancouver Marxist-Leninist Center, in which the Partisans would obviously be playing the leading role, ought actually to be leading all of CPC(M-L)'s Western Zone (everything west of Ontario), and, as added incentive, that the Partisan Central Committee should sit on the CPC(M-L) Central Committee. There could no longer be any doubt about the Partisan Central Committee's discovering the authenticity of CPC(M-L) as the true leadership of the Canadian proletariat!

The bandwagon got rolling in full force. The Partisan Central Committee figured out that the Partisan Organization was actually already a party of the vanguard Party, it was in fact just its "unorganized tendency" while CPC(M-L) was its "organized tendency". Members of the Central Committee led the various sections of the organization in struggle over the proposed merger, and easily quashed the objections (circulated in writing) of one Partisan member. Rathwell and certain other Central Committee members made certain that Paterson was kept in the dark about what was going on. (Rathwell was in danger of losing his leadership position in any case because of the time-wasting and politically questionable federal election campaign – Paterson might well have decided he was more needed in Vancouver and returned to replace Rathwell. Even more immediate was the probability that Paterson would have taken the next plane to Vancouver to burst the bubble, had he known what was going on with CPC(M-L). On October 29th the Partisan Central Committee summed up struggle and "unanimously decided to liquidate itself and all its outstanding work", declaring:

From this point on, there will be no distinction between Partisan work or the Partisan tendency apart from the consolidation of the Marxist-Leninist center of a new type. Concretely, this means that all previous notions of the Partisan's consolidating itself as a political tendency somehow independent of the new center should be rejected and repudiated as cultist and as remnants of circle spirit.

The "Marxist-Leninist Centre of a New Type",
publicly announced on November 4th, was just another
of CPC(M-L)'s euphemisms: nothing more than a
name designed to make things seem to be more than
they were, to people both inside and outside the
"Party". The Partisans immediately applied for
membership in CPC(M-L), and the "Marxist-Leninist
Centre of a New Type" was never anything more than
the Vancouver Branch of CPC(M-L). Bains, however,
had other plans for the Partisans: he was about to
wage a struggle to regain control of CPC(M-L), and he
needed energetic and capable revolutionaries with him
in the East to help him, particularly to put out the
Party's voluminous publications (including a daily
newspaper).

Two weeks after the formation of the Vancouver
Marxist-Leninist Centre, Bains had everyone from
Vancouver (as well as from other cities across Canada)
shipped to Toronto to a Party Conference, at which he
called on all cadre to oust the "bourgeois reactionary"
leadership at all levels of the Party and to reinstitute
his "proletarian line". The (former) Partisans
enthusiastically accepted this challenge, and at that
time went through a membership evaluation
procedure. Bains ripped off most of the former
primary and secondary leadership of Partisan to join
him indefinitely in the East, leaving the Vancouver
Branch with little strong leadership.

And that was the end of the Partisans: they were
physically dispersed, enmeshed in a reactionary
organization whose politics they were unable to

evaluate, and automatically viewed any criticism of CPC(M-L)'s politics and methods of work as manifestations of the "bourgeois reactionary line" (internally) or as slanders of the "Holy Alliance" of the New Left (externally). Ideologically, the Partisans had become extremely backward, with minds responsible only to the CPC(M-L) leadership.

Paterson flew to Vancouver right after the November CPC(M-L) conference in order to find out what was going on, and was surprised (to make an understatement) to find few of his old comrades still around. One former Partisan naïvely did set up a meeting between him and the members of the "New Marxist-Leninist Centre", but the Vancouver Branch leadership quickly cancelled it. There was nothing Paterson could do, and he returned to Toronto.

Conclusion

How could it happen? How could Partisan, having transformed itself into an organization moving off a basically sound, if somewhat sketchy, set of Marxist-Leninist principles, have suddenly committed hari-kari *en masse*? There certainly were fortuitous circumstances which immediately brought about the demise of the Partisan Organization: a strong counterrevolutionary "Maoist" organization eager to swallow up any burgeoning Marxist-Leninist opposition; a leader whose complete dominance was threatened by his political errors, who was not averse to using deception to maintain his career and who in any case was not politically competent to evaluate the competing organization; a complaisant leading body even politically less competent that the leader, always ready to follow his leadership in order to maintain their own positions. But while these essentially external factors were undoubtedly important *conditions* for the change, we know that we must look to internal factors for the cause, the *basis*, of the change.

As pointed out in the second section of this paper, during the summer of 1972 Partisan had transformed itself into a Marxist-Leninist organization in form only, not in content. With the exception of Paterson, way off in Toronto, neither the leadership nor the rest of the membership had any real understanding of Marxism-Leninism political theory; worse yet, they knew enough about Marxism-Leninism to delude themselves in thinking that they understood it well and had only to apply what they did know in order to carry out successful practice. The "Statement of Direction" of August 20th was a reasonable start for such an organization, but it contained errors and omissions and in any case was not internalized by the membership. For example, Partisan did not yet understand the relationship between the proletariat and the vanguard Party (or pre-Party formation), considering the Party to emerge from the proletariat as its "conscious, tested leadership"; this economist error ("workerism") was ruthlessly exploited by the Central Committee in arguing in favor of joining CPC(M-L) as the revolutionary vanguard which in fact had set itself up independent of the masses and which was (apparently) applying Marxist-Leninist theory throughout its work.

Without a solid grounding in Marxist-Leninist political theory, the Partisans easily fell prey to CPC(M-L) – the organization was outwardly Marxist-Leninist, but its members had not yet reached that level. This was the contradiction, between form and content, which caused the demise of Partisan. And while the case of Partisan was extreme, it certainly was not unique. Our movement abounds with Marxist-Leninist organizations with theoretical level not high enough to prevent their turning into their opposite – in the U.S., the Communist Party (Marxist-Leninist) provides one theoretical level of all their members, through systematic study of and struggle over the Marxist-Leninist classics and contemporary works. Cadre must become competent to evaluate the political lines coming down from leadership, and the organization must function in a way which allows effective struggle against erroneous positions taken by leadership. It is only in this way that a national Marxist-Leninist organization carrying out a correct political line can be built.

In view of the reactionary role played at the end by most of the Partisan Central Committee, one may ask whether it is not perhaps bad in general for leadership to be so "strong", in the sense of being able to impose its political lines on the whole organization. It is of course bad for leadership to impose incorrect political lines on the organization, but the rectification for this is not making leadership structurally weak (*e.g.*, by not allowing leadership to advance its positions in struggle within lower bodies, as was attempted during the struggle to rectify

Partisan's political line). In the case of Partisan, it was "strong" leadership which transformed it from a New Left organization to a Marxist-Leninist one. Central leadership, composed of the most theoretically advanced members of the organization, must always have the ability to "impose" correct lines on the organization (normally through protracted struggle, of course); to deny this is to deny the primacy of political theory in determining the practice of the organization. The rectification for a situation in which leadership is "strong" and membership is "weak" is, through systematic study, to raise the theoretical level of membership to the point where they are able to challenge incorrect political lines rather than just passively accepting them.

After two months, I finally thought I saw what was going on and attempted to struggle head-on against CPC(M-L)'s reactionary politics and methods of work. Having been a former Partisan Central Committee member, I had zealously supported the liquidation of Partisan, but had not been consciously involved in Rathwell's manipulations; and Bains had judged me not to be suitable to join him in the East. As a member of the Vancouver Branch of CPC(M-L), I deduced that the branch was "completely under the domination of the bourgeois reactionary line", and I wrote and managed to distribute among my comrades a twelve-page paper criticizing the branch's work in detail and proposing a course of rectification, in order to uphold "Comrade Bain's proletarian line". My paper was thoroughly trashed at a Branch meeting which refused to allow me to respond to criticisms of it, and I was roundly denounced by my former comrades. (Naturally, all copies of the paper were confiscated by the Branch leadership at the end of the meeting.) Undaunted, I flew to Montréal to present my case to a higher Party body, but I finally figured out, after banging my head against the wall enough times, that I had really been attacking CPC(M-L) as a whole, and that in fact the organization was controlled by the police. Through the struggle I had made no preparations to leave CPC(M-L), so when I did quite I was able to pull out only two other former Partisans (including my first wife) with me.

APPENDIX D: The **Washington State Rainbow Coalition**

First, an excerpt from Section c of Chapter 1 of
Beyond Classical Marxism:

One political experience in Seattle worth relating concerns the Rainbow Coalition initiated in the 1980's by Jesse Jackson. In the aftermath of the 1988 presidential election, the Washington State Rainbow Coalition was formed with about 1000 members. I was elected the state Corresponding Secretary, joining seven others to comprise the WSRC Executive Committee. On March 3, 1989 I attended a meeting of the National Rainbow Coalition in Chicago as an invited representative of the WSRC. There Jackson laid out a plan, which was duly approved, to essentially transform the state Rainbow chapters into his personal campaign committee. The new National Rainbow Coalition was to be a completely top-down organization, with the NRC president (Jackson) able to appoint and remove chapter officers, determine the operating procedures of chapters, and reorganize, suspend, or terminate any state or Congressional District chapter. I don't begrudge Jackson's wanting to convert the Rainbow Coalition for personal use, for he had created the organization in the first place, but what was abhorrent was the reaction of the WSRC leadership to this travesty of democratic functioning in what we were hoping to build.

As soon as I got back from Chicago, I gave a written report to the WSRC Executive Committee which explained in full detail what Jackson was intent on doing. To my amazement, there was no stated opposition (except mine) to the planned transformation of the National Rainbow Coalition. One ExCom member even stated that she would never circulate my report to *her* constituents! (She was a member of the Communist Party, but I don't believe any of the other ExCom members were in socialist organizations.) The ExCom evidently didn't want to do anything about the coming transformation of the WSRC, so I did the only honorable thing: as Corresponding Secretary, I maintained the organization's mailing list, so I mailed out my report to the officers of all the chapters. This action didn't bode too well with the ExCom (sorry, my bad!), but amid the furor there was nothing they could do but hold an organization-wide meeting to discuss the matter. At that meeting they presented a majority report and I countered with a detailed minority report, and I had managed to spike the liquidation of the WSRC into Jackson's transformed National Rainbow Coalition.

And here is the aforementioned minority report:

REPORT TO THE WSRC MEMBERSHIP ON THE
MARCH 3, 1989 NRC BOARD OF DIRECTORS MEETING
By Dave Jette, WSRC Corresponding Secretary
March 25, 1989

WHAT HAPPENED

On March 3, 1989 I attended a meeting in Chicago of the Board of Directors of the National Rainbow Coalition (NRC), as an invited representative of the Washington State Rainbow Coalition (WSRC). A major topic of this meeting was the organizational restructuring of the NRC, and a complete new set of bylaws was indeed adopted, as proposed by the Board of Directors' ad-hoc Restructuring Committee. The essence of this restructuring is to transform Rainbow into a campaign organization for Jesse Jackson's 1992 Presidential bid, and the NRC is now organized in a completely authoritarian, top-down fashion, instead of becoming the democratic, grassroots-based membership organization which most of us had been hoping for and even expecting.

According to the newly adopted NRC Bylaws, the NRC Board of Directors is a self-perpetuating body, electing one-third of its members every year on a rotating basis. Membership in the NRC is open to individuals and organizations (without any distinction between these two categories), and such membership is regarded as being of the "supporting type" – *i.e.*, dues-payers. National conventions of the NRC are to be held every four years, but apparently without any real decision-making power – the NRC Board of Directors is the ultimate authority.

The following points of the NRC Bylaws impinge directly on the democratic functioning of State Chapters:

1. The State Chapter's highest officer is the State Chairperson (or Co-Chairpersons). This person(s) is appointed by the NRC President (*i.e.* Jesse Jackson) in consultation with the NRC Board of Directors or the NRC State Chapters Committee (itself appointed by the NRC Executive Committee). The State Chairperson(s) may be removed at will by the NRC President.

2. The State Chairperson, acting in consultation with the NRC State Chapters Committee and the applicable State Leadership (for that state), may appoint such other officers of the State Chapter or of any Congressional District (CD) subchapter in a manner to be determined by the State Chairperson acting in consultation with the (NRC) State Chapters Committee and the (NRC) State Leadership Council. (Use of elections in this process is explicitly permitted, as an option.) The State Chairperson also establishes and appoints members of state leadership councils, steering committees, etc.)

3. Nevertheless, the NRC President, acting in consultation with the NRC State Chapters Committee and the applicable State Chairperson, "may appoint additional officers or remove officers of the State Chapter or any CD chapter thereof whenever such action is deemed to be to be in the best interests" of the NRC.

4. The State Chapters don't determine their own operating procedures. Rather, the NRC Board of Directors or the NRC State Chapters Committee, in

consultation with the NRC President, establishes these regulations, which the State Chapters and the officers and members thereof must adhere to.

5. State Chapters, CD subchapters, and Committees and officers and members thereof shall seek prior approval from the NRC Board of Directors, the NRC Executive Committee, or the NRC President before publicly taking any positions or endorsing any candidates in the name of or on behalf of the NRC or any State or CD Chapter thereof.

6. The NRC President, acting in consultation with the NRC Board of Directors, may reorganize, suspend, or terminate any State or CD Chapter "in the event such action is deemed to be in the best interests" of the NRC. The State Chairperson can appeal this action to the NRC State Chapters Committee. (Lots of luck!)

7. State conventions are called (only) by the NRC Board of Directors, in consultation with the State Chairperson. Like national conventions, these state conventions appear to have no real decision-making power.

In summary, the NRC has now been organized along the lines of a "campaign model", as it was termed at the March 3rd meeting. What is considered to be primary is organization discipline, so that the NRC will march lockstep in advancing Jesse Jackson's political career.

HOW WE SHOULD RESPOND

Let me continue this report by giving my own ideas on how we should respond to the NRC's organizational restructuring. First, we should be clear on what our relationship presently is to the NRC. In a word, this relationship is formally nonexistent. The WSRC is an organization, not yet incorporated under the laws of Washington State, which formed on February 11, 1989 under a set of bylaws (our "operational procedures") which we adopted at that time. Our bylaws give two legally interchangeable names for us: the "Washington State Chapter of the National Rainbow Coalition" and the "Washington State Rainbow Coalition". However, calling ourselves a chapter of the NRC doesn't make us that. Unless and until we modify our bylaws, we are governed solely by these bylaws, and in fact our bylaws state that they can be modified by the WSRC State Steering Committee only by a 3/4-majority vote, to meet the requirements of the NRC. This may well happen, but for the present we are governed by, and only by, the bylaws which we have democratically adopted. So there is no need to panic about the NRC's restructuring – we are not going to be governed by the campaign model unless we ourselves decide to accept it.

The question which lies before us is how – and whether – to apply to the NRC for state chapter status. In my view, our answer to that question should derive from two basic criteria:

(A) The top-down campaign model is completely unacceptable to us. Our vision of the Rainbow is of people's self-empowerment through building a mass-based organization advancing progressive politics through both electoral and nonelectoral activity. Such a grassroots political movement can be built organizationally only through complete internal democracy, so that people take up the struggle as their own rather than being external to themselves. Our democratic functioning is nonnegotiable.

(B) At the same time, we understand Jesse Jackson's need to build a campaign organization for his 1992 Presidential bid, and we acknowledge the tremendous inspirational role which he has provided, in building the Rainbow movement. While Jesse is not the embodiment of the Rainbow movement, he is by far its most articulate spokesperson, and we should strive to further his political career as much as possible, within the context of building the Rainbow movement in Washington State. Thus we should seek to work as closely as we can with NRC, while not giving up our own democratic functioning.

With these two criteria in mind, I should like to propose an approach to developing a relationship with the NRC. As our first preference, we should seek to join the NRC as a state chapter while retaining our present bylaws, making clear to the NRC that the campaign model is unacceptable to us. (It is quite possible that the NRC, faced with the nonacceptance of its top-down structure by a number of strong state Rainbow organizations, will find a way to accept us as we are, perhaps through "grandfathering".) If this doesn't work, the NRC may well accept us as an "organizational member" rather than as a state chapter;

this would be contingent upon our accepting and cooperating with a separate Washington State chapter to serve as Jesse Jackson's campaign organization here.

Finally, the NRC may adopt an antagonistic attitude toward us, and have nothing to do with us so long as we don't accept their campaign model of organization. In that case, we shall be faced with the decision of whether to carry on on our own (perhaps in association with other Rainbow activists across the country) or to disband. But let us try to avoid having to make this decision, and instead seek as close and mutually supportive a relationship as possible with the NRC, while retaining our completely democratic organizational functioning. This would be the ideal way to continue building the Rainbow movement in Washington State.

WHY THIS IS A MINORITY REPORT

In preparing for this meeting to report back to the membership on the NRC's restructuring, the WSRC Executive Committee (consisting of the eight newly elected WSRC officers, at present) formed a four-person subcommittee to draft a presentation of its views on how to deal with the NRC. These views are being expressed in this meeting in the form of a draft letter to the NRC, and in an oral report by the WSRC President. After continued struggle within the Executive Committee and within this subcommittee, I have found myself unable to agree with the approach of the majority towards dealing with the NRC, and I am therefore presenting this minority report. It should be made clear, however, that all of the Executive Committee who have been meeting together find the authoritarian character of the NRC's restructuring repugnant and desire to have it changed. In my view, the approach of the majority of the Executive Committee is principled and arguable, but wrong in certain fundamental ways. At issue, concretely, is whether the WSRC should tell the NRC clearly that its undemocratic procedures relating to the functioning of state chapters are unacceptable to us.

Let us be frank. The organizational restructuring of the NRC is not some sort of aberration, some inexplicable departure from the norms of democracy which guide practically all grassroots organizations in this country. The NRC has been restructured for a particular purpose: to destroy Rainbow as an independent, mass-based progressive political organization which can effectively challenge the status quo (or rather, to prevent its developing into such an organization, for the Rainbow is still organizationally in its infancy). There are extremely powerful forces operating at the national level of Rainbow which seek to push back into the bottle the genie of progressive politics which has been called forth by Jesse Jackson's two presidential campaigns. This is why Rainbow has never developed a democratic national structure, why we were told not to hold our founding convention in the aftermath of last June's Democratic National Convention, not to hold it in the aftermath of the 1988 presidential election, and even not to hold it last month. The

March 3rd restructuring of the NRC constituted the consolidation of control of Rainbow by these conservative forces.

So what should we do in this situation? Those of you who have read my original (March 6th) report to the WSRC Executive Committee on the NRC's restructuring, will see that my first reaction was to call for our having nothing to do with the NRC so long as it was governed by these outrageous bylaws. But I now do agree with the rest of the Executive Committee, that we should seek to develop as close a relationship with the NRC as possible, consistent with maintaining our own completely democratic functioning. The question is, how do we do this?

I think there is no alternative to laying our cards on the table and saying, politely but firmly: this is what we are, we would like to work closely with you, but under no circumstances will we accept such undemocratic procedures as appointment or removal of officers from above. If, in requesting state chapter status, we pretend that our bylaws are consistent with NRC's, we are going to be continually pressured to place into positions of leadership persons who accept the NRC's authoritarian structure – this will be the deliberate policy of the forces who now control the NRC. (This is already happening, concerning making a certain person a co-chair of the WSRC.) At each point we will look for compromises, rationalizing that in the future we shall be stronger and better able to resist, but in the end we shall wind up with an organizational structure which is democratic in name only. If the forces now in control of the NRC will not accept us now as a completely democratic organization, they will surely not accept such blasphemy in the future, when they have consolidated themselves and weakened the democratic forces within Rainbow.

Even more important is the question of where our source of strength lies: with our relationship to the NRC, or with our membership? There is no doubt that Jesse Jackson has played a tremendous inspirational role in creating the Rainbow, but it is we – our membership at every level – who have built the WSRC. And we have built the WSRC through two basic factors: our progressive politics, for which there is such a need in this country; and our democratic functioning, which enables all our members to take up the struggle as *their own*. Completely democratic functioning is absolutely essential to building a progressive mass-based movement, for there are such powerful forces working against us that we have got to actively involve and rely upon all our members. But how can we keep, or even attract, members when in practice we consider our relationship to the NRC to be more important than our democratic functioning? How can we present ourselves to the people of Washington State as building a grassroots movement when we tremble in fear at challenging the NRC's authoritarian structure? Whom do we really represent?